Salient Features of
Indian Astrology

Prof. U.C. Mahajan

(Author of 'Lal Kitab' & 'Horoscope Reading Made Easy')

PUSTAK MAHAL

Publishers
Pustak Mahal®

J-3/16 , Daryaganj, New Delhi-110002
☎ 23276539, 23272783, 23272784 • *Fax:* 011-23260518
E-mail: info@pustakmahal.com • *Website:* www.pustakmahal.com

Sales Centre
■ 10-B, Netaji Subhash Marg, Daryaganj, New Delhi-110002
☎ 23268292, 23268293, 23279900 • *Fax:* 011-23280567
E-mail: rapidexdelhi@indiatimes.com
■ Hind Pustak Bhawan
6686, Khari Baoli, Delhi-110006
☎ 23944314, 23911979

Branches
Bengaluru: ☎ 080-22234025 • *Telefax:* 080-22240209
E-mail: pustak@airtelmail.in • pustak@sancharnet.in
Mumbai: ☎ 022-22010941, 022-22053387
E-mail: rapidex@bom5.vsnl.net.in
Patna: ☎ 0612-3294193 • *Telefax:* 0612-2302719
E-mail: rapidexptn@rediffmail.com
Hyderabad: *Telefax:* 040-24737290
E-mail: pustakmahalhyd@yahoo.co.in

© **Author**
ISBN 978-81-223-0993-5
Edition: 2011

Printed at : Param Offsetters, Okhla, New Delhi-110020

Introduction

Let me confess that till 1996, I was a novice and knew nothing about the fundamentals of Astrology. I requested some of the astrologers of the town to teach me the basics of Hindu Predictive Astrology, but to my utter dismay, they all dissuaded me from venturing into the field which had given nightmares to even the greatest of astrologers. But I remained undaunted and kept on reading books on this 'Ancient Science of Prediction' in Urdu, English and Hindi. Today, after a lapse of about ten years, I can claim to have 'some', if not 'complete' knowledge of the subject.

I know that none except God is infallible; but an astrologer who is imbued with a love for this science and welfare of human beings at heart, can relieve the sufferings of the people with certain astrological remedies. Today, even the doctors, who were earlier sceptical about the efficacy of such remedies, heal their patients with astrological charts. Let me reiterate that I have cured many patients with these remedies; even doctors will vouch for my assertions.

My aim in writing this series is to apprise the people of the finest nuances of astrology and to prove that it is not 'humbug' or 'hoaxology', as vociferously suggested by certain people who claim that they are out to destroy such 'false myths' and 'superstitions'. Let me confidently say that astrology is a time-tested science. It is the most precious heritage of ours. We may err, but astrology never goes wrong. The fault, dear Brutus, lies in us, and not in this "Science of Gods".

Let me pay my homage to my revered parents Late Shrimati Maya Devi and Lala Ghamir Chand Kaistha {of Mohalla Porian, Sujanpur Tira, Distt. Hamirpur (H.P.)}. They are blessing me from heavens. I still have my ancestral house in Himachal Pradesh. Let me also express my love to my wife Sudarshan Mahajan and my children Rajiv, Sanjeev and Sandeep, their spouses Nirupma, Manisha and Shivali and my grandchildren Karan, Neha, Apoorva, Akshit and Arsh, my brothers, friends and well-wishers.

I also take this opportunity of expressing my thanks to my publishers – M/s Pustak Mahal, Daryaganj, New Delhi, and its team of professionals associated with production for publishing my books on astrology.

Suggestions will be thankfully acknowledged and incorporated in the next edition.

— **Prof. U.C. Mahajan**

Contents

INDIAN ASTROLOGY

Chapter 1 What is Astrology and What are its
Advantages 09

Chapter 2 Horoscope or Birth Chart 12

Chapter 3 Planets 18

Chapter 4 Houses 25

INDIVIDUAL PLANETS

Chapter 5 Sun (Surya) 35

Chapter 6 Jupiter (Guru) 38

Chapter 7 Moon (Chandra) 41

Chapter 8 Mars (Mangal) 44
(Exalted and Malefic)

Chapter 9 Venus (Shukra) 47

Chapter 10 Saturn (Shani) 50

Chapter 11 Mercury (Budh) 53

Chapter 12 Rahu 55

Chapter 13 Ketu 58

PLANETS IN RAASHIS

Chapter 14   Sun (Surya)... 63

Chapter 15   Jupiter (Guru).. 65

Chapter 16   Moon (Chandra)...................................... 68

Chapter 17   Venus (Shukra).. 71

Chapter 18   Mars (Mangal)... 74

Chapter 19   Mercury (Budh)....................................... 77

Chapter 20   Saturn (Shani).. 80

Chapter 21   Rahu.. 83

Chapter 22   Ketu... 86

Chapter 23   How to Read a Birth Chart........................ 89

Chapter 24   Debilitating or Inauspicious Planets.............. 91

Chapter 25   Important Lessons 93

Chapter 26   Mahadasha Calculation 96

Chapter 27   Varsh Phal.. 112

Chapter 28   Diseases Caused by Malefic Planets............ 123

Chapter 29   Some Prominent Yogas............................... 129

Chapter 30   Gems and Precious Stones 135

Chapter 31   Overview and Charts for Quick Reading.... 141

————————❖◆❖————————

Indian Astrology

CHAPTER 1

What is Astrology and What are its Advantages

Let me quote the greatest scientist of the 20ᵗʰ century – Albert Einstein:–

"Astrology is a science in itself and contains an illuminating body of knowledge. It taught me many things and I am greatly indebted to its geophysical evidence. It reveals the power of the stars and the planets in relation to the terrestrial. In turn, astrology reinforces this power to some extent. This is why astrology is like a **Life-giving Elixir** to mankind."

Astrology indeed is a 'Divine Amrita' or 'Life-giving Elixir' and I need not quote any other critic in support or against this "Science of Stars". When the greatest scientist of the world vouchsafes for the significance of astrology, it is futile to comment upon the observations made by pigmy detractors of this 'Divine Science'.

Definitions of Astrology:

It is rightly believed that the movement of the planets – Sun, Moon, Mars, Venus, Saturn – do affect the lives of human beings inhabiting this Earth. Have we not heard of the phrase: "**As above so below**"?

In simple words, it means that the stars make or mar our lives. If we are born under a "Lucky Star", we rise high in life; whereas an ill-starred person leads a miserable life. But it should be remembered that these heavenly forces have no personal ill-will against us. They are impersonal and they can be appeased through certain remedies, for their enmity is transient. As they move on, they change their positions every now and then, and even the so-called malefic planets become benefic and vice versa.

I have seen great men falling to lowest depths and small ones rising to great heights. There is a Persian phrase:–

> *"Her Kamale Ra Zawale;*
> *Her Zawale Ra Kamale."*

Those who have risen must fall and those who have fallen must rise. History is replete with instances of the rise and fall of various empires.

Certain Instances:

(i)   Julius Caesar was warned by a soothsayer to beware of the 'Ides of March', i.e. 15th March. He did not pay heed to this prophecy and was killed on that day.

(ii) Louis XVI of France was warned by an astrologer to be on his guard on the 21st of every month. He took this advice to heart and resolved not to embark upon any journey or do important business on that day. But alas! Hounds of Fate overpowered him on that date. He and his queen were arrested on June 21, 1791, while they were fleeing, and on January 21, 1793 they were guillotined, i.e. executed.

(iii) Rasputin, the Mad Monk of Russia, was told by Cheiro in 1905 that he would meet a violent death within the palace and that he would be menaced by poison, by knife and by bullet. He could see in his vision the waters of Neva closing above the monk. On December 29, 1916 this prophecy come true. Even Rasputin himself had predicted his own death, the ultimate doom of the Czar's empire and the commonisation of the nobles.

(iv) Sardar Patel's death was predicted by a soothsayer nine months before it occurred. Satya Narayan Singh, then a Central Minister, informed Sardar Patel of the ultimate tragedy. The great Sardar fobbed him off, but the prophecy was correct and Sardar Patel passed away on that very day as was predicted.

(v) A godman had predicted the unceremonious exit of T.T.Krishnamachari, former Finance Minister. He had also predicted Maulana Azad's fall in his bathroom and death four days later. T.T.K. was forced to resign from the Union Cabinet, despite Nehru's protests. Maulana Azad fell in his bathroom and lost consciousness. Dr. B.C.Roy was asked to treat Azad but to no avail. After four days Maulana Azad died.

(vi) The astrologers had also predicted the death of Veerapan, the smuggler-king of Tamil Nadu and Karnataka. Instances galore about the predictions made by soothsayers.

It is true many predictions go wrong, but that does not prove its detractors right. Exception does not prove the rule. Such sceptics dismiss all these predictions and prophecies as mere coincidences.

Let me conclude with a statement by R.C. Smith:–

"Let us get this straight. It is not prophecy. It is dealing not with certainties, but with tendencies. It has a fairly wide margin of error; but it works." This Universe is like one organised body. Mankind and the cosmos are inter-linked with a rhythmic harmony, and that is why we say the planets play a vital role in human affairs. But there is, however, one snag:– **" We cannot change the course of destiny though we may be able to foresee the coming events."**

————————❖◆❖————————

CHAPTER 2

Horoscope or Birth Chart

For a soldier, the most important equipment is his gun; similarly, in order to arrive at the exact conclusion, the astrologer needs the following equipments:

(a) Date of Birth

(b) Time of Birth

(c) Place of Birth

(d) Longitude and Latitude of the place of birth.

Note: Accurate timing is crucial. A baby's first cry is usually taken as the moment of birth.

The reader can easily prepare the Birth Chart with the help of 'Panchangs' (ephemerides). Computerised horoscopes are also available.

Preparation of Birth Chart:

One must have basic knowledge as to how the traditional Hindu astrologer prepares the Birth Chart. He takes into consideration Sun's entry into Aries (Mesh) or 13th April or 1st Baisakh (i.e. beginning of the month of Baisakh in Hindu calendar).

Raashi No.	Name of Raashi	Duration of Sun per Raashi per day	Month (Hindu Calendar)	Month (English Calendar) Approximate dates
1	Aries (Mesh) (3 Ghatis)	72 minutes	Baisakh	13 April to 12 May
2	Taurus (Vrisha) (4 Ghatis)	96 minutes	Jeth	13 May to 12 June
3	Gemini (Mithun) (5 Ghatis)	120 minutes	Ashar	13 June to 12 July
4	Cancer (Kark) (6 Ghatis)	144 minutes	Sawan	13 July to 12 Aug
5	Leo (Singh) (6 Ghatis)	144 minutes	Bhadon	13 Aug to 12 Sept
6	Virgo (Kanya) (6 Ghatis)	144 minutes	Asuj	13 Sept to 12 Oct
7	Libra (Tula) (6 Ghatis)	144 minutes	Kartik	13 Oct to 12 Nov
8	Scorpio (Vrishchik)	144 minutes (6 Ghatis)	Marg-shirsh	13 Nov to 12 Dec
9	Sagittarius (Dhanu)	144 minutes (6 Ghatis)	Posh	13 Dec to 12 Jan
10	Capricorn (Makar)	120 minutes (5 Ghatis)	Maagh	13 Jan to 12 Feb
11	Aquarius (Kumbha)	96 minutes (4 Ghatis)	Phagun	13 Feb to 12 March
12	Pisces (Meen) (3 Ghatis)	72 minutes	Chaitra	13 March to 12 April
	Total	**1440 Minutes (24 Hrs) (60 Ghatis)**		

Note: Astrologers mention Ghatis and Pals instead of minutes. Here is the table for conversion into minutes and hours.

(a) One Ghati is equivalent to 24 minutes and 60 Pals make one Ghati.

(b) 2½ Ghatis = one hour

(c) 60 Ghatis = 24 hours (one day)

Raashis (Signs):

I have mentioned Raashis (Signs) in the preceding pages. Now the question arises as to what is Raashi and what are their names and functions.

As the planets and Moon move in roughly the same plane, they seem to keep to a certain region of the sky, making up a belt known as 'Zodiac'. Thus Zodiac is an imaginary belt in the heaven, divided into twelve equal sections or signs or Raashis (Ras in Urdu), each named after a constellation (group of stars). These are (i) Aries (The Ram) (ii) Taurus (The Bull) (iii) Gemini (The Twins) (iv) Cancer (The Crab) (v) Leo (The Lion) (vi) Virgo (The Virgin) (vii) Libra (The Scales) (viii) Scorpio (The Scorpion) (ix) Sagittarius (The Archer) (x) Capricorn (The Sea Goat) (xi) Aquarius (The Water Bearer) and (xii) Pisces (The Fish).

Each Raashi covers 30 degrees and the whole circle is completed by $12 \times 30 = 360$ degrees. To be precise, Aries covers first 30 degrees; Taurus from31-60°; Gemini from 61-90°;Cancer from 91-120°; Leo from 121-150°; Virgo from 151-180°; Libra from 181-210°; Scorpio from 211-240°; Sagittarius from 241-270°; Capricorn from 271-300°; Aquarius from 301-330°; and finally Pisces from 331-360°. Thus the circle of Zodiac (Raashi Chakra) is complete.

Let me write down the Hindi names of these Signs (Raashis or Ras) and their Lords, etc.

Raashi No.	Name of Raashi	Colour & Nature	Symbol	Lord of Raashi	Part of Body	Exalted Planet	Most Malefic or Worst Planet	Bringer of Luck
1	Aries (Mesh)	Red & Fiery	Ram (Mendha)	Mars (benefic)	Head	Sun	Saturn	Mars
2	Taurus (Vrish)	White (curd-like)	Bull (Baail)	Venus	Neck & Throat	Moon	Nil	Moon
3	Gemini (Mithun)	Green & Windy	Couple (Jorra)	Mercury	Shoulders & Arms	Rahu	Ketu	Mercury
4	Cancer (Kark)	Milky white & Watery	Crab (Kekra)	Moon	Chest & Stomach	Jupiter	Mars	Moon
5	Leo (Singh)	Copper red & Fiery	Lion (Singh)	Sun	Heart, Lungs & Liver	Sun + Jupiter	Nil	Sun

6	Virgo (Kanya)	Green coloured & Earthly	Girl	Mercury & Ketu	Belly & Intestines	Mercury + Rahu	Ketu	Mercury + Rahu
7	Libra (Tula)	White (curd) & Windy	Scale (Tarazu)	Venus	Back-bone & Marrow	Saturn	Sun	Venus
8	Scorpio (Vrish-chik)	Blood red & Fiery	Scorpion (Bloody Scorpio)	Mars (malefic)	Kidney & Genitals	Nil	Moon	Moon
9	Sagittarius (Dhanu)	Yellow & Fiery	Cow & Archer	Jupiter	Thighs	Ketu	Rahu	Jupiter
10	Capricorn (Makar)	Black & Earthly	Sea goat or croco-dile (mag-armach)	Saturn	Knees	Mars	Jupiter	Saturn
11	Aquarius (Kumbh)	Black & Windy	Water bearer or pitcher (Gharra)	Saturn	Legs	Nil	Nil	Saturn + Jupiter
12	Pisces (Meen)	Blue + Yellow & Watery	Fish (Machhali)	Jupiter & Rahu	Feet	Venus + Ketu	Mercury + Rahu	Ketu

Summary of the above:

1. Lord of Aries (1) and Scorpio (8) is Mars (benefic) and Mars (malefic) respectively.

2. Lord of Taurus (2) and Libra (7) is Venus.

3. Lord of Gemini (3) and Virgo (6) is Mercury.

4. Lord of Cancer (4) is Moon.

5. Lord of Leo (5) is Sun.

6. Lord of Sagittarius (9) and Pisces (12) is Jupiter.

7. Lord of Capricorn (10) and Aquarius (11) is Saturn.

8. Lord of Virgo (6) is jointly with Mercury and Ketu (malefic).

9. Lord of Pisces (12) is jointly with Jupiter and Rahu (malefic).

Senard, a Western astrologer, says that these twelve signs of the Zodiac are the sum total of four **Elements** (earth, water, air and fire) multiplied by three **Gunas** or modes, referred to in the

[15]

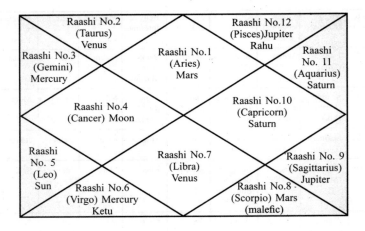

Holy Geeta, viz; "Sattva, Rajas and Tamas". Sattva is superior, Rajas is transitional and Tamas is vile and base. Thus 4 × 3 is equal to 12. He also interprets these signs as under:

S.No.	Name of Sign	Attributes
1	Aries	Urge to create and change for the better
2	Taurus	Magnetism which attracts all
3	Gemini	Imagination
4	Cancer	Child in the womb; period of gestation and then birth of the child
5	Leo	Individual identity, will power; indomitable courage
6	Virgo	Intelligence
7	Libra	Equilibrium; balance
8	Scorpio	Breakdown of organic tissues
9	Sagittarius	Coordination and joining parts to make a harmonious whole
10	Capricorn	Asceticism or self discipline
11	Aquarius	Illumination; splendour; brightness
12	Pisces	Mystic fusion; direct intercommunion with God; state of spiritual ecstasy like "Pranayama"

Planets and Their Tendencies and Attributes:

S.No.	Name of Planet	Tendencies & Attributes
1	Sun	Will & potential activity
2	Moon	Imagination
3	Jupiter	Good learning, judgement, teaching & right direction
4	Saturn	Power of endurance and reserve
5	Venus	Love & family relationship
6	Mars	Action & destruction
7	Mercury	Intuition & movement

CHAPTER 3

Planets

Now let us talk of planets whose movements in heaven affect the lives of individuals on this Earth. Don't we say that "**stars do govern our condition**".

Here are the names and functions of planets which affect human life:

1. **Sun (Surya):** It is the central force of the Solar System. It is the King Emperor that rules over the body and soul and all other planets obey his commands. It is the supreme source of light and life. If exalted it brings glory and fame; and if weak or malefic it brings misery. A man with an exalted Sun is born to rule and the one with a weak Sun is born to serve. In Hindu mythology, we call it Lord Vishnu who is the Lord of the Universe. In Islamic astrology, it is called 'Shams' or 'Khurshid' in Persian. His height is normal; has a bright face; both the hands raised and are 'Lion' like. Its main period lasts for 6 years.

2. **Jupiter (Guru):** He is the great 'Guru' or the teacher, preceptor and guide of the gods. If exalted the man becomes learned; scholarly, specialist in languages and pious and noble, but when malefic, man becomes a poor sadhu and is reduced to utter poverty like Sudama in Hindu mythology. He is Lord Brahma of the Hindu Trinity of gods and is the creator of the Universe. Its main period lasts for 16 years in a cycle of 120 years.

In Islamic astrology, he is called 'Mushtri' or 'Barjis'– an old venerable man with a book in his hand.

3. **Moon (Chandra):** She is the Lord of the mind, heart and eyes and sea travels. She is the Mother Earth showering all the blessings on her children. If benefic, it bestows all wealth and comforts, filling the ocean of life with abundance of milk and wealth. But if malefic, it makes the man insane, psychic, who may even commit suicide. Its main period lasts for 10 years in a lifecycle of 120 years. In Islamic astrology, it is called 'Qamar' or 'Mah' in Persian; the picture of a tall man with both hands on his shoulders with a halo around his face.

4. **Mercury (Budh):** It is the most powerful planet, though a eunuch. If friendly it bestows all favours. It is the most deadly enemy if malefic. Man with benefic Mercury is well-read, jolly and liberal; and one with weak or malefic Mercury is a flatterer who indulges in meaningless talk. According to Hindu mythology, it is all-powerful Goddess Durga. Its main period lasts for 17 years in a life cycle of 120 years. In Islamic astrology, it is called 'Attaroo'. It is the picture of an old man with a long beard, carrying a pen in his hand and a piece of paper resting on the knees; as if he is writing something.

5. **Venus (Shukra):** It is a beautiful and sweet-tongued planet. It refers to marital happiness if exalted and discord if malefic. If exalted, it confers all pleasures on the spouse and if malefic, it is lustful and undependable. In Hindu mythology, it refers to Goddess Laxmi, the goddess of wealth and monetary well-being. Its main period lasts for 20 years in a life cycle of 120 years. In Islamic astrology, it is called 'Zauhara' or 'Naheed' in Persian. It is the picture of a beautiful woman with a musical instrument in her hand.

6. **Mars (Mangal):** When benefic it confers strength and power and relieves man of his pain and problems. If malefic, it wreaks havoc and spreads lawlessness and anarchy. It dances the dance of death. In Hindu

mythology, it refers to both the aspects of Lord Shiva– the Lord of happiness and bounty and the Lord of death. It is Lord Hanuman – the reliever of pain and destroyer of enemies. Its total period extends to 7 years in a life cycle of 120 years. In Islamic astrology, it is called 'Mariakh' or 'Behram' in Persian. It refers to the picture of a soldier carrying a sword in one hand and the slain head of the enemy in the other hand.

7. **Saturn (Shani):** It refers to a black cobra which stings and also the snake carrying 'Sapphire' (Mani) over its hood. If benefic, it confers all wealth and power. If malefic, it hisses, stings and injects poison. Its main period lasts for 19 years in a life cycle of 120 years. In Hindu mythology, it is referred to as Lord Bhairon or Lord Yama, the lord of the underworld. In Islamic astrology, it is called 'Zohal' or 'Kewan' in Persian. It is the picture of a man with long hair, six hands, carrying sickle in two hands striking at the donkey, a branch of a fruit tree in other two hands and the tail of a rat in the remaining two hands. It is all black in colour.

8. **Rahu:** Rahu is not a planet but a node called "Dragon's Head". If exalted, it confers power and position. It is like the trunk of the elephant which can take man to great heights, but a malefic Rahu throws the man into a gutter and slough of misery and poverty. It even throws the man into prison, whether innocent or guilty. In Persian astrology, it is called 'Raas'.

9. **Ketu:** It is a dog that leads the man to the hut of a dervish or sadhu. It also refers to son. If exalted, one is blessed with noble sons; if malefic; son goes astray and brings ignominy to parents. It is called "Dragon's Tail" and has no independent existence of its own. It acts as a slave to Rahu and acts at Rahu's dictates. In Persian astrology, it is called 'Zunab'.

10. **Uranus, Neptune and Pluto*:** These planets were discovered in 1781, 1846 and 1930 respectively. Astrologers studied thousands of horoscopes to assess

their influence upon human life. They ultimately allotted "Joint lordship" to these planets with the old ones. Uranus is now the joint lord of Aquarius (11th Raashi) with Saturn. Neptune shares it with Pisces (12th Raashi), i.e. Jupiter. Pluto shares it with Scorpio (8th Raashi), i.e. Mars. Modern astrologers are of the opinion that the effect of Uranus on Aquarius is stronger than that of Saturn; and that the effect of Neptune on Pisces (12th Raashi) is stronger than that of Jupiter. As regards Pluto's influence, nothing can be said with certainty. The traditional Hindu astrologers do not attach much importance to these newly discovered planets. I have referred to them just for academic discussion.

*   *Recent reclassification has written off Pluto as a planet. It is now a dwarf planet and has been assigned Asteroid number 134340. Let us forget about him and give him a decent burial. Our sages and ancient astrologers referred to the effect of 7 planets only and they have been proved right.*

Friendship, Enmity and Neutrality among Planets.

Just as nations and individuals have friends, enemies and neutral people, planets too have among themselves friends, enemies and neutral planets. Here is a chart showing friendship, enmity and neutral positions of planets.

S. No.	Planet	Friends	Neutral or Planet of Equal Power	Enemies
1	Jupiter	Sun, Moon & Mars	Saturn, Rahu & Ketu	Venus, Mercury
2	Sun	Jupiter, Moon & Mars	Mercury (Combust) & Ketu (bedims Sun) Surya Grahan)	Venus, Saturn & Rahu (Solar Eclipse,
3	Moon	Sun, Mercury	Saturn, Venus, Mars & Jupiter	Ketu (Lunar Eclipse, Chandra Grahan), Rahu (bedims Moon)
4	Venus	Saturn, Mercury, Ketu	Mars, Jupiter	Sun, Moon & Rahu
5	Mars	Sun, Moon, Jupiter	Saturn, Venus, Rahu (ineffective)	Mercury, Ketu

Contd...

[21]

6	Mercury	Sun, Venus, Rahu	Saturn, Ketu, Mars, Jupiter	Moon
7	Saturn	Mercury, Venus, Rahu	Ketu, Jupiter	Moon, Sun, Mars
8	Rahu	Mercury, Saturn, Ketu	Jupiter, Moon (bedimmed)	Venus, Sun (Solar Eclipse), Mars
9	Ketu	Venus, Rahu	Jupiter, Saturn, Mercury, Sun (bedimmed)	Moon (Lunar Eclipse), Mars

Please study the above chart carefully. You will notice that some planets love others, but their love is spurned and rejected. What a strange situation!

1. Mercury befriends Moon, but Moon opposes Mercury.

2. Venus does not oppose Moon, but it is Moon who hates Venus. That is why whenever Moon-Venus are together in the horoscope, we find estranged relationship between the mother-in-law (Moon) and daughter-in-law (Venus).

3. Jupiter and Venus are of equal strength but it is Venus who opposes Jupiter. Jupiter is a learned teacher, but not rich and Venus is a beautiful woman who would prefer a rich man to a poor man of scholarship. Hence this strange relationship; as Jupiter loves Venus but his love is not returned.

4. Mars and Saturn are of equal strength, but it is Mars who opposes Saturn.

5. In House no. 2, Jupiter dominates Rahu who vows to shun his evil ways.

6. Although Moon and Mercury are enemies, yet in House no. 2 and 4, they give up their enmity and help each other.

7. It may be noted that the planets which harbour ill-will and hatred suffer, but not the other. Moon opposing Mercury suffers but not Mercury.

Exalted and Malefic Planets:

Planets in their own Houses and Raashis are exalted; whereas planets in enemy Houses and Raashis are the most debilitating.

The former brings glory, wealth and fame; and the latter brings poverty and misery. Here is the chart:

	Sun	Moon	Mars	Jupiter	Mercury, Saturn	Venus
Exalted Raashis	Aries (1)	Taurus (2)	Capricorn (10)	Cancer (4)	Libra (7)	Pisces (12)
Malefic Raashis	Libra (7)	Scorpio (8)	Cancer (4)	Capricorn (10)	Aries (1)	Virgo (6)

Aspects of Planets (Drishtis):

1. 100% aspects:

House no.1 aspects House no.7; House no. 8 aspects House no.2; House no. 3 aspects House no.9; House no. 4 aspects House no. 10; House no.5 aspects House no.11; House no.6 aspects House no. 12 and vice versa. If the planets are so aspected by a friendly planet, the results are good, otherwise bad.

2. 50% aspects:

It is a friendly aspect even though aspected by an enemy.

House no.1 aspects House no.5; House no. 2 aspects House no.6; House no. 3 aspects House no.7 and 11; House no. 4 aspects House no. 8; House no.5 aspects House no.9; House no.6 aspects House no. 10; House no.7 aspects House no.11; House no. 8 aspects House no.12; House no. 9 aspects House no.1; House no. 10 aspects House no. 2; House no.11 aspects House no.3; House no.12 aspects House no. 4.

3. 25% aspects:

House no. 2 aspects House no.12; House no.8 aspects House no.6.

Special aspects:

100% aspect: All planets including Rahu and Ketu; **7th aspect**.

Jupiter 100% aspect: 5th, 7th and 9th.

Mars 100% aspect: 4th, 7th and 8th.

Saturn 100% aspect: 3rd, 7th and 10th.

[23]

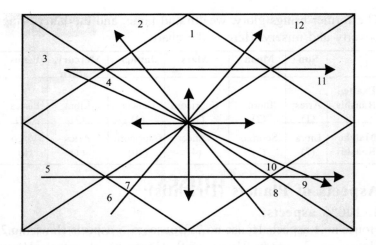

The aspects are very important. Suppose any enemy planet is in House no.8, it will lose its sting if Mars is in House no.5 or Jupiter is in House no.4. In that case, House no.8 is aspected and protected by its Lord or the most benefic planet.

Houses

The **12 Houses** form the most important section of the Horoscope. Each House has its own distinctive nature and function. These Houses are permanent ones and influence the life of an individual in the most remarkable way.

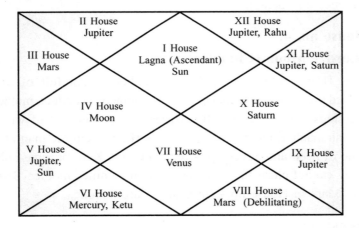

House no. 1:
{Lagna or Ascendant; Lord – Sun (Surya)}:

It is the most important House in the Birth chart. It governs body, soul, name, fame, glory, character, age, head, brain, aspirations, personality, etc. If occupied by an exalted planet, it brings name and fame and if it is malefic, it brings misery and loss of name and wealth.

House no. 2:
{Lord – Jupiter (Guru)}:

It is the temple of God and sacred dwelling place of 'Great Guru'. It refers to domestic happiness, personal fate and old age. It is one of the most important Houses. Even the sinful 'Rahu' vows to shun its evil ways in this House. Every planet in the House becomes exalted and planet of fate, if House no.8 is vacant. It represents gold, silver, nose, eyes, ears and beauty.

House no. 3:
{Lord – Mars (Mangal)}:

This House refers to relatives, brothers, illness, short travels, writing, etc. and is also the road to the other world. It is also an outlet for wealth. Moon in this House confers life and saves man from death and misfortunes. It also represents courage, patience and breath.

House no. 4:
{Lord – Moon (Chandra)}:

This House refers to education, mother, ocean full of milk, landed property, conveyance, treasure, righteous conduct, mother's blessings, abundance of all luxuries, parents and lot of wealth, and stomach ailments. Planets in this House help the man at the time of need and adversity. Even Rahu and Ketu become noble. They cannot cheat the mother as Moon signifies mother. Saturn and Mars in House no.4 (in Cancer) are malefic.

House no. 5:
{Lord – Sun and Jupiter (Surya and Guru)}:

It refers to children, knowledge, learning, future of children, intelligence, education, wisdom, eminence, writing of books, etc. Malefic Saturn and malefic Venus exercise bad effect on this House, but that effect is reduced to a great extent if Moon is exalted in the horoscope.

[26]

House no. 6:
{Lord – Exalted Mercury and Weakest Ketu (Budh and Ketu)}:
This House refers to the underworld presided over by Lord Yama (the god of death); maternal uncles; enemies, secret help, litigation, work, servants, food, sickness and worries, ailments of anus and uterus. Ketu, though the joint Lord of this House, is debilitating (worst effect); whereas Mercury gives the best effect.

House no. 7:
{Lord – Venus (Shukra)}:
This House refers to domestic happiness or discord; marriage; husband's or wife's love for each other; sexual desires – pure or lustful – affairs with other woman too; passion, desire for perfumes. It is, in fact, the House of Goddess Laxmi (the goddess of wealth). It causes piles, etc.

House no. 8:
{Lord – Malefic Mars (Bad Mangal, most debilitating)}:
It refers to death, disease and justice – tit for tat; longevity of life; disease of sex organs, bad name, violence, bad fate, etc. Scorpio is the symbol of death and disease.

House no. 9:
{Lord – Jupiter (Guru)}:
It refers to inheritance, rich legacy and landed property; noble actions, piety, pilgrimage and visit to holy places; long life of parents, foundation of one's fate. An exalted Jupiter confers name, fate, royal status and wealth.

House no. 10:
{Lord – Saturn (Shani)}:
It is the field and foundation of fate and actions; means of livelihood, profession, position, father's blessings, trade and general success in life. Mars in this House is the most exalted; whereas Jupiter is the weakest. If this House is destroyed by enemies through adverse aspect; it becomes a 'blind horoscope' – very bad indeed.

House no. 11:

{Lord – Saturn (Shani) in the Durbar of Jupiter (Guru)}:

It refers to foundation of fate, House of income, gains, acquisition of gold, profit, fulfilment of aspirations; speculations, friendship, etc. It is the House of acquisition of wealth and House no. 3 is the outlet for spending that wealth. Exalted planet, especially Saturn in this House becomes planet of fate whereas the malefic planet brings misery when it occupies House no. 1 in the Annual chart (11, 23, 36, 48, 57, 72, 84 etc.). Further, malefic planet in this House becomes the planet of deception, disaster and adversity, if it occupies House no.8 in the Annual chart (7, 20, 34, 45, 53, 67 etc.). Exalted Mars in this House confers wealth and eminent status provided House no.2 is occupied by a male planet.

House no. 12:

{Lord – Jupiter (Guru) and Rahu (malefic)}:

This House refers to conjugal bliss, financial loss, expenditure, hour of death; imprisonment, bad name, mental torture, grief, dreams, etc. This House is the final authority on all appeals.

Certain Examples:

To elucidate my contention about Raashis and Houses, let me cite a few instances:

Birth Chart:

Example no. 1:

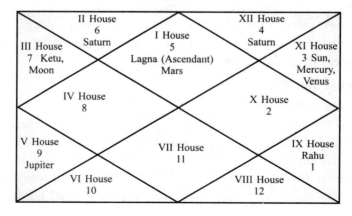

Let there be no confusion about **Raashis** and **Houses**. We find that House no.1 (Sun's House) is occupied by Mars (Sun's friend) in Sun's Raashi (Raashi no.5). It has conferred exalted status on the individual who is a high ranking officer and is a writer of repute. Jupiter in 5th House (in its own and Sun's House) in its own exalted Raashi has made him rich. He is a gentleman par excellence. Moon is exalted but is destroyed by Ketu, its sworn enemy. He remains tense on account of imaginary fear. Sun, Mercury and Venus in 11th House are benefic. Only Saturn in Cancer makes him tense in mind, because Saturn destroys Moon in Cancer.

Example no. 2:

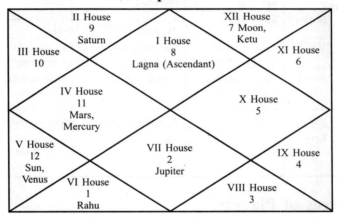

Here Saturn is very exalted. It confers wealth, authority and a lot of property. Mercury in 4th House is exalted. Mars makes him 'Manglik' but being in Aquarius confers wealth and property. Sun in 5th House makes him a teacher in the college/university. Venus in Pisces confers all marital pleasures. Jupiter is weak; hence he suffers from bronchitis, but serves his father well. Moon and Ketu, though exalted, keep him under tension for nothing. Ketu has blessed him with eminent sons.

More Information about Planets: Attributes concerning Planets:

S.No.	Planet	Nature (Human relationship)	Time	Articles to be donated, if malefic
1	Sun	Self	8:00 AM to 10:00 AM (Sunday)	Wheat, jaggery & copper
2	Moon	Mother, mind, heart	10:00 AM to 11:00 AM (Monday)	Rice, milk, silver
3	Jupiter	Father, gold, teacher	6:00 AM to 8:00 AM (Thursday)	Saffron, gold, turmeric
4(a)	Mars (exalted)	Brother	11:00 AM to 1:00 PM (Tuesday)	Masur daal, red things
4(b)	Mars (malefic)	Man-eater, destroyer	11:00 AM to 1:00 PM (Tuesday)	Masur daal, red things
5	Mercury	Sister, aunt	4:00 PM to 6:00 PM (Wednesday)	Moong, green things
6	Venus	Lover, beloved, wife, husband	1:00 PM to 3:00 PM (Friday)	Ghee, curd, white butter
7	Saturn	Parental uncles & son opposed to father	Saturday night	Urad, iron, leather goods, coal & timber
8	Rahu	In-laws	Thursday evening	Mustard (sarson)
9	Ketu	Son, dog	Sunday early morning blanket	Sesame (til), white & black

Degrees of Planets:

. Please do not jump to conclusion if Mars is in 8th house in Scorpio. It is true that it is the most malefic but find out its degree. If it is at 29 or 30 degrees, it is a dying planet; hence its effect is almost negligible. Similarly, it is just an infant if it is at 1 or 2, or 3 degrees. Similar is the case with other planets – good or bad.

Degree	Planet is a
3 to 9 degrees	Child
10 to 22 degrees	Young & very powerful
23 to 28 degrees	Middle aged, sliding towards old age
29 to 30 degrees	Dying planet
1 to 2 degrees	Just born

Chart showing Friendly, Enemy or Deceiving aspects of Planets:

House No.	Mutual friendly 50% aspect	Basic aspect 100%	Enmity aspect (8th aspect)	Deception (10th aspect)	Sudden loss or injury, etc.
1	5	7	8	10	3, 7 & 11
2	6	-	9	11	4
3	7 & 11	9	10	12	1
4	8	10	11	1	6 & 10
5	9	11	12	2	7
6	10	12	1	3	4
7	11	1	2	4	1, 5 & 9
8	12	2	3	5	10
9	1	3	4	6	7
10	2	4	5	7	4, 8 & 12
11	3	5	6	8	12
12	4	6	7	9	10

Note: Please study the above chart carefully:

(1) Mutual friendly 50% aspect: Every planet, even enemies, will help each other (50%) at the 5th aspect.

(2) Enmity aspect (8th aspect): Every planet even though friendly, will destroy the planet at the 8th aspect. Example: Jupiter in 10th house will destroy even exalted Sun (a great friend in 5th house).

(3) Deception (10th aspect): Deceiving planets means it can be good or bad. Sun in House no.2 will bring unexpected wealth and glory when it occupies House no.11 in Annual chart. Similarly, malefic Moon or any other malefic planet in House no.3 will bring misery and depression when it occupies House no.12. Thus deception can be both good and bad.

[31]

(4) Sudden loss or injury, etc.: Malefic planet in House no.1 leads to accident or loss when it occupies House no.3, 7 and 11. Similar is the case with other planets, occupying House mentioned therein.

❖◆❖

Individual Planets

Sun (Surya)

An exalted Sun confers glory, brightness, long life. Such a man is truthful, will never face bad days, will earn a lot; even death will lose its sting.

1. **Sun in House no. 1:** Very wealthy, king-like status, self-made rich. Handsome in body, thoughts and soul; honest; intellectual; liberal; justice-loving; helpful to father; strict administrator, but should be a polite businessman. Early morning birth; short-tempered; long life.

2. **Sun in House no. 2:** Wealthy; good reputation; good status; God-fearing; pious and noble; bright and glorious life; selfless service will bring about exalted results.

3. **Sun in House no. 3:** Bold like a lion; long life of mother provided Moon is exalted; rich in old age; good to gentlemen but harsh to evil-doers or liars.

4. **Sun in House no. 4:** Very rich; beneficial travels abroad; exalted status, will be frugal himself, but will leave millions for children; will have lots of wealth to donate even pearls; the more large-hearted he is, the better the results; perfect Raj Yoga; lustful conduct will, however, destroy him.

5. **Sun in House no. 5:** Bringer of good luck; a perfect gentleman; excellent government job; if exalted, best

results; and if malefic, worst results; like a bright lamp shedding light everywhere; the older he grows, the richer he is.

6. **Sun in House no. 6 (Raashi effect):** Such a person is like King Nero, rejoicing at the destruction of his kingdom; no worry about job, may leave one but get another; but short-tempered; in spite of failures will never stoop low; care-free like Don Quixote (Śheikh Chilli).

7. **Sun in House no. 7 (Worst Raashi effect):** Everything goes topsy-turvy; like a king himself responsible for the loss of his crown and kingdom; unlucky; short-tempered; rude, selfish; prone to flattery; rich but not wise; couple should be faithful for better results.

8. **Sun in House no. 8:** Conqueror of death; good position; even Mars in House no.8 will not be debilitating; for better luck be affectionate to his elders; must not be lustful; death fears Sun in this House.

9. **Sun in House no. 9:** Long life; supporter of family members; most glorious Sun; man of honesty and integrity; will do everything for family and will not demand any favour in return. Even House no.5 becomes exalted. Best placement in the Birth chart provided it is not aspected by enemy planets, i.e. Rahu, Saturn, Ketu, etc.

10. **Sun in House no. 10:** Healthy, wealthy but superstitious; will be underestimated though very intelligent; competent officer; will never bow before tyranny; self-respecting; sincere friend. If alone, it brings bad results regarding inherited property.

11. **Sun in House no. 11:** Noble and religious-minded; long and happy life; greedy because of **Saturn's** effect; the nobler in deeds and thoughts, the more eminent the status; must not touch wine.

12. **Sun in House no. 12:** Enjoys sound sleep, but worried about others; happy couple; lively, knowledgeable; honest; worst results if lustful and corrupt; bad luck if he deals in machines (Saturn's trade), but good luck in investment and other types of business (Mercury's trade).

Note: Sun, if in conjunction with Rahu, Saturn, and Ketu and adversely aspected by them, brings about worst results. It is in fact **eclipsed**.

❖◆❖

Jupiter (Guru)

1. **Jupiter in House no. 1:** If exalted and man is educated, he enjoys king-like status; may be a scientist or doctor doing research; scholarly; bringer of good luck for parents at the age of 16 years and himself becomes famous in old age. Exalted service, status, prosperous; victory over enemies; good-natured but short-tempered; age not less than 75 years; bold like a tiger. If malefic, person is a famous sadhu, but poor.

2. **Jupiter in House no. 2:** Temple of God, where 'Great Guru' resides; exalted position; best government job; wealth, promotion and property come to him without any effort; will inherit property; noble, pious, hospitable, rich, provided House no.8 is not vacant. If malefic, person brings disaster and misfortune on the family.

3. **Jupiter in House no. 3:** A sincere friend, but a deadly foe. If Mars is exalted, such a person is just and fair in his dealings; intelligent, wise; comfortable life; very powerful and brave. If Mars is malefic, such a person is a coward, unlucky and quarrelsome; will be a terror for others and will rob others' wealth and property.

4. **Jupiter in House no. 4:** Grand house; foundation of wealth; ocean full of milk; seat of justice; wealthy;

tranquillity of mind; full of fortitude and courage during bad times; smiling face; compassionate; Goddess Laxmi smiles upon him; beautiful spouse and obedient children; in fact, the best planet. If malefic, worst fate; will be responsible for his own doom and family's destruction, especially when Rahu and Ketu are bad, and is aspected by Venus, Saturn and Mercury from House no.10.

5. **Jupiter in House no. 5:** Exalted status; rich after birth of a son; enjoys respect and esteem; short-tempered yet noble and large-hearted.

6. **Jupiter in House no. 6 (Raashi effect):** Parasite, enjoying at other's expense; will get everything effortlessly; prosperous maternal uncles, but not helpful. If malefic, life full of sorrows and sufferings.

7. **Jupiter in House no. 7 (Raashi effect):** Asthmatic; sadhu in previous birth; unhappy with brothers and sisters; rise after marriage; late birth of a son; may settle away from relatives; bad investments but leader of family and well-to-do.

8. **Jupiter in House no. 8:** Philanthropist; rich; long life; have blessings of ancestors and God's blessings too. If Mars is malefic, a poor sadhu living in a graveyard.

9. **Jupiter in House no. 9:** Most exalted planet; rising fortune; interest in spiritualism; very rich fore-fathers; noble and royal wealth and lineage; upholder of family values. If aspected by both Venus and Moon, life full of ups and downs.

10. **Jupiter in House no. 10:** Worst results; loss of money; disruption in studies; receives nothing from parents in life and even after their death; intelligent but does not get his due; Must not indulge in lustful acts. Very bad from 27-36 years of age, but good after that.

11. **Jupiter in House no. 11:** Lonely like a palm tree; like gilded gold; if good to others, he will be fortunate; worst

fate after father's death; father leaves nothing for him; should be noble and religious-minded for best results. Sisters will be thankless; he himself will be a coward. If lustful – worst fate, even shroud will be provided by strangers at his death.

12. **Jupiter in House no. 12:** The more he earns, the more he should donate. Lots of money; a competent adviser; a yogi full of kindness and love; blessed with divine feelings. If malefic, man will not be able to use his own wealth though rich.

———————❖◆❖———————

Moon (Chandra)

1. **Moon in House no. 1:** Purity of heart; mother's blessings; wealthy; long life; success in service matters. Must respect his mother for best luck; money spent on education will not go waste. If malefic, must not sell milk and must not take bribe.

2. **Moon in House no. 2:** Most exalted planet; bringer of best luck; self-made rich; eminent position; happiness from parents; will receive inherited wealth. Marriage in a wealthy family; will receive education with mother's blessings.

3. **Moon in House no. 3:** Lord Shiva protects the person from death and destruction, loss and theft; fountain of goodness; wealthy; long life; good for meditation and devotion. If Mars is malefic, mother will oppose him or vice versa.

4. **Moon in House no. 4:** Most exalted planet; ocean of milk; wicked planets even bow before the mother and give up their evil ways. Must donate milk and keep his temper cool; good old age; successful in ancestral business; must complete his education.

5. **Moon in House no. 5:** Beautiful like a bird; bird of good omen; fountain of pure milk, honest, truthful, soft spoken, polite; wealthy and must live abroad. Justice-

loving and helpful to others; intelligent. Moon is asleep if House no.9 is vacant (must take sweets before doing auspicious work). If malefic, man may use foul language and is an unsuccessful traveller over jungles and hills.

6. **Moon in House no. 6 (Raashi effect):** Complete Lunar eclipse; good to those who are good to him and bad to evil-doers; believes in tit for tat. Moon, if alone bestows all luxuries in youth. When malefic, it may adversely affect the parents (especially mother) in their life and health.

7. **Moon in House no. 7 (Raashi effect):** Best placement; very rich; incarnation of goddess of wealth if not aspected by enemies; expert astrologer; intelligent; must not quarrel with mother; will enjoy all comforts, respect and esteem everywhere. If malefic, must donate milk, rice and silver; should not accept gifts of silver, milk, etc.

8. **Moon in House no. 8:** Worst; but bringer of good luck; long life; may suffer from epilepsy, fits and swoons; but will have children; must not deal in jewellery. If malefic, then most unfortunate, insane; life full of troubles; problems of heart, brain and eyes.

9. **Moon in House no. 9:** Precious jewel in the family; polite, humane, good-doer; noble. A perfect gentleman; may travel abroad. If malefic, life full of ups and downs likes a sandy desert.

10. **Moon in House no. 10:** Like poisonous and sour milk; Moon is meaningless in this house; must shun lustful conduct for better results; enmity with mother will spell doom; but long life. May earn a lot as a surgeon; disruption in education.

11. **Moon in House no. 11:** In this House Moon is zero, i.e. worst. It is like milk without butter; life full of storms. However, if it is in exalted Raashi, it gives best results.

12. **Moon in House no. 12:** Prone to flattery; face like that of a white cat; dreamer dreaming of past glory; like river in flood destroying inherited property and wealth; but self-created wealth will help; bathing with rain water will help. If Jupiter and Sun are exalted, results will be good.

------------◆◆◆------------

Mars (Mangal)
(Exalted and Malefic)

1. **Mars in House no. 1:** If exalted, it is the sword of justice – army or police officer; resourceful; exalted status; fair and just. If malefic, such a person is like a falling star; unfortunate, evil-minded; bringer of misfortune on all.

2. **Mars in House no. 2:** If exalted, may receive property from in-laws; rich, having all comforts; leader of family; will help all. If malefic – such a person is like a snake eating up his own family; unfortunate; quarrelsome; may die in a fight. But if Mars and Ketu are together in the House – good results.

3. **Mars in House no. 3:** If benefic, such a person is a tiger in a zoo, i.e. meek like a deer; happiness from friends and relatives; Lord Shiva's blessings; just and fair; expert in martial arts; good eye. If malefic, notorious, cheat and a fraud; but coward; luxurious life at other's expense; ill-fated; hated by all; bad for business too.

4. **Mars in House no. 4 (Raashi effect):** Worst effect on himself and family members; a devil in human form; like an ocean on fire; may bring death and destruction for all; may suffer from disease of throat and navel; even honey turns into poison; lord of death; diseased; cruel; picks quarrels; malefic Mars (in Cancer and

Scorpio) is 'Manglik' and may spell death, disaster and loss of life and property. Remedy lies in **Moon** – donate milk, silver and rice.

5. **Mars in House no. 5:** If exalted, such a person gets happiness from wife and children; wealthy; man of knowledge and scholarship; the older he grows, the richer he is; just and fair; ancestor of rich and eminent children and grandchildren. If malefic, notorious; fear of fire; bad eyesight; enmity with all; his beloved may cause destruction.

6. **Mars in House no. 6 (Raashi effect):** If benefic, a contented sadhu; religious minded; sweet-natured; will rise high in life; a great writer; noble; bringer of good luck to brothers too. If malefic, bad fate; rioter and instigator; foul-mouthed.

7. **Mars in House no. 7:** If benefic, supporter of family; happy family life; noble; good adviser; lots of wealth and property; good status; competent administrator. If malefic, unfortunate; accursed; unfaithful wife; lustful conduct; bad character; illicit relations with loose character women.

8. **Mars in House no. 8:** If benefic, man is hard-working; just and fair and will face everyone boldly. Mars in this House is the worst, but if House no.2 is vacant or occupied by Sun, Jupiter or Moon, then Mars will no longer be 'Manglik' or Mars negative. If Mercury is benefic, Mars gives the worst results. This House is the death trap or noose of the gallows; worst results till 28th year. If Sun or Moon or Jupiter is in House no.4, this House will not be House of death; wound or burn mark on body. Worst and most malefic Mars in this House.

9. **Mars in House no. 9:** The most exalted planet; bringer of best luck for parents on birth, then at 13-14th year and will himself have king-like status at 28 years of age. Royal birth; wealth and authority. If malefic, such a person is a notorious atheist. Bad financial condition of parents, if Mercury is debilitating in House no.12.

[45]

10. **Mars in House no. 10:** Most exalted; king-like position, if alone and not aspected by enemy planet; bold like a tiger; lots of property; all pleasures of life; very rich. Eminent status, provided House no.2 is not occupied by a female planet. Life is all sweet like honey. If malefic, he will sell his gold and will be destroyed; interested in black magic and tantra.

11. **Mars in House no. 11:** Like a red ruby in the family; a tiger commanded by Jupiter, best placement; rich; noble and helpful to all; comfortable life; king-like status at 28th year. Exalted Jupiter makes it doubly exalted. If malefic, worst fate; always under debt though rich; uncomfortable life; unhappy with children.

12. **Mars in House no. 12:** If exalted, Mars is the competent and expert rider riding the elephant (Rahu). Rahu becomes ineffective and is controlled by Mars. Traditionalist; man of words; given to self-praise; respectful to elders; all comforts. If malefic, asthmatic; bad domestic life; bad eyesight (night blindness); loss of wealth; unnecessary and foolish expenditure.

——————❖◆❖——————

Venus (Shukra)

1. **Venus in House no. 1:** It is both good and bad in this House; man / woman of extreme temperament; will fall in love without consideration of status, caste and even creed; will sacrifice all for the lover; may lose his heart and soul to the lover or even paramour. If malefic, ill-health of wife; loss of his own health and wealth; but all comforts.

2. **Venus in House no. 2:** If benefic, God's blessings on the couple. Wealthy; will have plenty of everything; best domestic life; exalted personal fate; victory over enemies. If malefic, wife / husband will be incapable of producing a child; may suffer from anaemia or sexual weakness; may have to adopt a child; lustful conduct will spell ruin.

3. **Venus in House no. 3:** Venus will confer best results; faithful and loving spouse; wife is tigress in temper, but a coward; wife is a source of inspiration; will stand by him through thick and thin. He must love her and remain faithful to her, otherwise she will dominate him and he will have to remain meek and humble before her. If Mars is benefic, Venus will bestow good results, otherwise bad.

4. **Venus in House no. 4 (Raashi effect):** Life will be fine and good for 4-5 years after marriage, thereafter discord between mother-in-law and daughter-in-law.

Lustful conduct and illicit relations with loose character woman / man will bring ruin.

5. **Venus in House no. 5:** House full of children; if noble, best results; love for land, family and birth place; will never lose his job till wife's life. If lustful, worst results on self, and not on wife and children.

6. **Venus in House no. 6 (Worst effect):** Good for nothing man; impotent man; barren woman. If woman is loved and respected, man will prosper, otherwise will lose all; eunuch; like a sparrow; unreliable woman. Insulting attitude towards all, even for elders and friends; flattery of women; but good health and eyesight. When Venus in no.6 is malefic, the person may do foolish things and may even donate his all but God protects him; skin troubles; even deprived of the affection of his wife.

7. **Venus in House no. 7:** Most exalted planet; 'though one-eyed', it confers all comforts, pleasures and benefits; noble and faithful spouse. Lustful conduct will spell doom and destruction. Business with in-laws will result in loss.

8. **Venus in House no. 8 (Worst effect):** Short-tempered spouse; domineering attitude; will always have her say; must pray in a temple, mosque or church. Must not accept bribes and must not marry before 25 years of age.

9. **Venus in House no. 9:** Rich ancestor, but bad for children; may have to work hard for earning his livelihood; though intelligent and a competent officer; even if he is rich, will have to work hard. If malefic, life full of storms; may have to spend a lot on wife's health.

10. **Venus in House no. 10:** If Saturn is exalted, best results; noble; faithful wife; one may dream of beautiful woman or may make love to another woman; one must be of good character. In youth a lover, but a preacher in old age. Must be of good character and must not be lustful.

11. **Venus House no. 11:** Lots of wealth; but effeminate; prone to allergy of skin; lack of sexual urges; outwardly simple but very clever like a snake; wavering mind; beautiful wife; handsome man, keen to earn more and more.

12. **Venus in House no. 12:** Most exalted planet if in Pisces; faithful wife; bringer of good luck; confers all pleasures and comforts – whether domestic or sexual. Good luck after marriage; fond of music, poetry, etc. Exalted status in service; victory over enemies. Best placement indeed. When a man passes through bad times, wife inspires him; serves his family; all pleasures from wife but not vice versa. If wife suffers from ill-health, husband should bury blue flower in a deserted place.

❖◆❖

Saturn (Shani)

1. **Saturn in House no. 1:** Most malefic; worst fate; dishonest, cheat; liar; like a dry wood eaten by termites; worst results regarding wealth and property; long but wretched life. Must not be lustful and must not be addicted to wine and vices. Sun's effect will however be good – case of 'father helping the bad son'.

2. **Saturn in House no. 2:** If benefic, it confers wealth, lands and property; benefic snake at the feet of the master; outwardly simple but very clever and intelligent; competent officer; merciful, just and fair; exalted status; leader among men and colleagues. If malefic, in-laws will be destroyed after marriage; but Jupiter (father) will be helpful.

3. **Saturn in House no. 3 (Raashi effect):** Long life, if not lustful, otherwise the worst planet. Bad relations with brothers. If benefic, an expert eye specialist but must give free medicines to the needy and the poor. If malefic, relatives will be responsible for his downfall.

4. **Saturn in House no. 4:** If benefic, one may be a doctor; shrewd and clever; four-eyed man; things related to Saturn will be helpful. If drug addict, he will write his own doom. A malefic Saturn is like a water snake; may suffer till 36ᵗʰ year.

5. **Saturn in House no. 5:** Worst scenario; like a snake eating its own children; cheat but poor; subtle like a

snake; ill-health and troubles; involvement in litigation. Saturn in Sun's House and in Leo is the most malefic.

6. **Saturn in House no. 6 (Raashi effect):** Most notorious; retrograde; stings even friends in House no.2; marriage after 28th year beneficial otherwise worst for mother and children. Malefic Saturn in House no.6, gives worst results, loss of shoes, machines, cars, etc. and may also face police case.

7. **Saturn in House no. 7:** Most exalted; income will run into lakhs; engineer or doctor; if Mars is exalted, eminent position in government, i.e. may be an I.A.S. officer. Very rich, owner of lands; humane; compassionate; from rags to riches. If he is drug addict or lustful, he will invite his own doom and may even face police case. If Mars is malefic, results will be bad.

8. **Saturn in House no. 8:** House of death; Saturn in its own burrow. It hisses and frightens. Even a dead snake sends creeps down the spine. A large growth of hair on chest indicates slavery; fear of death; bad eyesight in old age. Avoid wine at all cost.

9. **Saturn in House no. 9 (Raashi effect):** Best placement; rich; owner of three houses or even more; snake's hood with sapphire; well-read; kind-hearted, owner of lands; long-lived; comfortable life for self and children. Even Venus will become exalted; will have blessings of the parents.

10. **Saturn in House no. 10:** It is Saturn's own house; hence bringer of good luck; will be very rich with lots of property. Such a person should be cunning and clever like a snake, then he will get the regards of others; if he is noble and kind, he will be crushed by others; long life of father. He will receive all honour and wealth. If Saturn is malefic, i.e. in debilitating Raashi, such a person is like a stinging snake; blind horoscope – unfortunate and accursed; should be subtle and clever to face the poisonous arrows of fate. If gentle, he will meet his doom.

11. **Saturn in House no. 11:** Architect of his own fate; writes his own destiny; best planet for wealth, power and position; will have a son, will inherit wealth and prosperity; noble; religious-minded. If addicted to wine and drugs, worst results. Corruption and bribery will be disastrous.

12. **Saturn in House no. 12:** Bad domestic life; will never lack money and job; Lord Shiva's blessings; very rich; exalted status; victory over enemies. Must not be lustful; dishonest and corrupt. Must not be addicted to wine and drugs. Noble life will make him happy and prosperous.

––––––––––––❖◆❖––––––––––––

Mercury (Budh)

1. **Mercury in House no. 1:** Exalted position; administrator but selfish; best in girl's Birth chart. Even malefic planets lose their sting; more exalted than Sun in service matters; life of luxury but greedy; foul-mouthed if addicted to wine.

2. **Mercury in House no. 2:** Best personal fate; good for in-laws; witty; self-made rich; good writer; well-read; serve the family well; mother will live long; life of luxury and comforts. If malefic, problems in the birth of male child; bad investments; sisters, daughters and aunts may oppose him.

3. **Mercury in House no. 3:** Worst scenario; a leper to be shunned; bat hanging upside down; destroys House no. 4, 5, 9 and 11. Bad for others but good for self.

4. **Mercury in House no. 4:** Mercury in Cancer is the most exalted; lots of wealth; exalted service but restless and under tension; happy couple. Mother like a swan who has given birth to a precious jewel. Mentally active; perfect Raj Yoga; multi-millionaire.

5. **Mercury in House no. 5:** Man of great learning and knowledge; best for couples but bad for father; an expert and divinely gifted astrologer. Everything beautiful, good and full of wealth and happiness.

6. **Mercury in House no. 6:** Most exalted; liberal; Mercury acts as a loyal servant to the person; self-made rich; life is lovely and fragrant like a flower; good results of sea

travel; successful trader; writer and speaker; intelligent; owner of lands; honesty will reward him. All planets become exalted, if Mercury is best. If dishonest and corrupt doctor, he will be a loser; must shun ill-gotten wealth and corrupt ways.

7. **Mercury in House no. 7:** Will never be bad in girl's Birth chart, but in boy's horoscope, he will help others but remain where he is. Educated; good old age; good business; victory over enemies. A precious diamond for the family; age 80 years. Malefic Mercury will destroy both Mars and Venus.

8. **Mercury in House no. 8:** Worst fate; financial loss; poisonous; leper to be shunned; disease of teeth, veins and intestines. Loss of income; death trap; financial problems; loss in career; worst scenario indeed.

9. **Mercury in House no. 9:** A king who is afflicted with leprosy, i.e. who is discarded by all. Mercury in Sagittarius is the most debilitating and worst; ill-fated; short-lived even. If a person stammers in childhood, it may not be that bad but still it is the most debilitating.

10. **Mercury in House no. 10 (Raashi effect):** A flatterer leading a comfortable life but thankless and selfish; sly like a snake and cunning; planner, if Saturn is good and Mercury will confer good results, otherwise bad. Must not be addicted to drugs and must have control over his tongue and language.

11. **Mercury in House no. 11:** Very rich; a precious diamond; prosperous and rich after 34th year. If malefic, it will bring disaster; ill-mannered; worst results till 34th year.

12. **Mercury in House no. 12 (Worst Raashi effect):** Worst results; fate like that of a mad dog; sleepless nights; short-tempered; foul-mouthed; may run away; undependable; worst fate awaits him. Bad name; humiliation; loss of income and money; may face ignominy and imprisonment on account of alleged fraud, cheating, etc. But in woman's Birth chart it is not malefic.

❖◆❖

Rahu

1. **Rahu in House no. 1 (Raashi effect):** Rich, elephant (Rahu) making the man rich, but also throws him into slough of misery; complete Solar eclipse, i.e. man may lose his job, but will soon get another; will regain the earlier job status after eclipse is over. Minimum period of bad fate is between one and two years; will spend on households; man himself responsible for bad fate.

2. **Rahu in House no. 2:** Rahu shuns its wicked ways in this House. If Jupiter is exalted, Rahu bestows all comforts, otherwise bad financial conditions. A malefic Saturn makes it more deadly. If exalted, Rahu confers glory and exalted status on man; even if he is a sadhu, he will be a famous one; lot of expenditures; comfortable life. If malefic, ups and downs in life; may be charge-sheeted for alleged offences, but will never be arrested.

3. **Rahu in House no. 3:** Exalted Rahu bestows all authority, wealth and property; very rich; protects the man from enemies; sincere friend; liberal enemy; will be blessed with sons; enemies will go in hiding; will enjoy all promotion and comforts. If malefic, he will be cheated by ungrateful relatives.

4. **Rahu in House no. 4:** Noble, as Rahu bows before Moon – the mother; rich; religious-minded; but bedims Moon, i.e. full of tension and imaginary fears regarding wealth and drowning. After the eclipse, Moon will regain brightness.

5. **Rahu in House no. 5:** Notorious; not a good placement for sons; if exalted, it may confer all comforts and benefits. But if malefic, one may have to spend on illness; bad for domestic peace.

6. **Rahu in House no. 6:** Most exalted; elephant conferring all pleasures, wealth and property; intelligent; victory over enemies; self-respecting and proud. If malefic, a notorious thief; mad elephant killing its own master.

7. **Rahu in House no. 7:** Rich but bad domestic life; good status but unhappy with wife and in-laws. In girl's horoscope may lead to divorce; unlucky; lustful conduct will ruin the couple.

8. **Rahu in House no. 8:** Planet of death; announces the message of death; life full of ups and downs; bitter and stifling smoke; a hypocrite; corruption will spell doom. Involvement in litigation; prone to accident; illness; loss of life even; it destroys health, wealth and life. Worst planet.

9. **Rahu in House no. 9:** Worst placement; most malefic; complete Solar eclipse for official career; but good after 42 years of age; bad fate; partial Lunar eclipse; lots of expenditure; may even destroy House no.5 – the House of children; dishonest; irreligious.

10. **Rahu in House no. 10:** If exalted, it is a precious sapphire. But if malefic, it is like a poisonous snake causing instant death. If Saturn is exalted, Rahu automatically becomes benefic. If Saturn is malefic, Rahu will cause ill-health, unnecessary expenditure, losses in wealth and destruction of property. Such a person is mean and jealous.

11. **Rahu in House no. 11:** A mere cipher till 36th year of age, i.e. no wealth, etc.; after his birth parents also suffer losses. But after 36th year, self-made rich and will not demand anything from parents and in-laws.

12. **Rahu in House no. 12:** Worst placement; a day dreamer; full of dirty imaginary ideas; mad elephant; unnecessary expenditure; may be involved in police cases; theft, embezzlement; may be imprisoned; sleepless nights; bad relations with family members and friends. An exalted Rahu, however, may mean rich in-laws but Rahu's effect will be malefic.

❖◆❖

Ketu

1. **Ketu in House no. 1:** Man having imaginary unfounded fears about children and job; will never lose job; if he loses one the other will be available; serves his father and teachers.

2. **Ketu in House no. 2:** Generous and liberal; rich but will spend a lot; mother may not like him but wife will respect and love him, i.e. loving and adoring wife; must not be lustful for better results.

3. **Ketu in House no. 3:** A sadhu; a good-doer; thankful to benefactor and forgives the enemy; helpful to all, especially the relatives who will be ungrateful and may slap court cases on him. No happiness from children even.

4. **Ketu in House no. 4:** Complete Lunar eclipse; tension; depression; noble, wise and religious-minded; bad for mother but not for father; full of wild thoughts; bad health – physical as well as mental.

5. **Ketu in House no. 5:** If of good character, he will be blessed with two sons; and Ketu's results will be the best. If lustful, he loses his beauty and youth and looks old even in youth; a lot of financial benefits; faithful to father.

6. **Ketu in House no. 6:** Worst; most debilitating; complete Lunar eclipse; but clever and shrewd; undependable;

coward and good for nothing; loses his confidence; large number of enemies who are out to harm him.

7. **Ketu in House no. 7:** If benefic, will earn a lot of wealth; victorious; a rich man; Ketu, like a faithful dog, will protect the master and pounce upon enemies; very lovable character. If an egoist, he will be a loser. Must not be short-tempered for happy domestic life; must keep his word.

8. **Ketu in House no. 8:** Worst; groaning and barking dog that scares away all; must not be lustful; may suffer from urinary troubles, boils, wounds, etc. Its effect will be still worse if House no. 2 is vacant.

9. **Ketu in House no. 9:** Best and most exalted; bringer of good luck for parents; may live abroad; self-made rich; the more the gold, the richer; most fantastic results regarding wealth, travels, etc.

10. **Ketu in House no. 10 (Raashi effect):** Rich; will never lose wealth. If Saturn is good, Ketu is doubly good; forgiving nature will help. If lustful, he will invite his own ruin. Must be of good character.

11. **Ketu in House no. 11:** Self-made rich provided Mercury is not in House no.3; learned; wise but jackal-like dog. Ketu's effect is exalted for the birth of son.

12. **Ketu in House no. 12:** Exalted; best placement; name and fame; best luck and wealth after son's birth; helpful to family; will have very rich and loyal sons. Everything will be fine regarding wealth and property; luxurious life.

———❖◆❖———

Planets
in
Raashis

Planets
in
Raashis

Sun (Surya)

1. **Sun in Aries:** Exalted; being in a friendly Raashi; short-tempered but an officer; if trader, must be soft-spoken. In a good House it gives best results; self-confident.

2. **Sun in Taurus:** In the 2nd, 5th and 9th Houses it confers best results. But Sun in 7th and 10th House is not good; remains disturbed because of enemies.

3. **Sun in Gemini:** In a friendly sign; will never be malefic; person will be of sweet and soft speech; wise and thoughtful.

4. **Sun in Cancer:** Best placement; very rich; mother's blessings; best luck. Earns name and fame.

5. **Sun in Leo:** Only son; eminent status; intelligent; wise and well-read; bringer of good fortune; short-tempered.

6. **Sun in Virgo:** No worry about job; problem with feet; may leave job many times; carefree.

7. **Sun in Libra:** Worst if in House no.7 or in enemy's House; unlucky; problem in service and marriage, being in enemy's Raashi; ill-tempered; rude and selfish. If honest to the spouse, good and comfortable life, otherwise worst.

8. **Sun in Scorpio:** Conqueror of death; death fears Sun; rich, promotion provided not lustful.

9. **Sun in Sagittarius:** Best planet; long life; best results regarding career, health and wealth. It brightens House no.5 too regarding sons.

10. **Sun in Capricorn:** Being in enemy's Raashi, such a person is full of wild and bad thoughts and is quarrelsome; wrong-doer; bad and deceitful behaviour like a stinging snake. But if it is in Sun's House, it confers good results.

11. **Sun in Aquarius:** It is also in the enemy's Raashi, hence selfish and full of deceit and evil thoughts. But in its own House, i.e. House no.1, it blesses the man with son and confers wealth and eminent status.

12. **Sun in Pisces:** Being in a friendly Raashi; man is wise and self-made rich; frugal and does not spend lavishly; spends a lot on household affairs; honest; owner of lands; a good-doer; purity of mind, thought and deeds.

————❖◆❖————

Jupiter (Guru)

1. **Jupiter in Aries:** Brings good luck to parents; recipient of all comforts, power; educated; researcher; can see through enemy's game; short-tempered; honest; man of integrity, optimist; large-hearted; good-doer; may earn name and fame; sometimes over liberal but at times stingy. It is a benefic placement, being in a friend's Raashi.

2. **Jupiter in Taurus:** Lover of good things; self-made rich. If in House no. 2, man will receive wealth and property from in-laws as well as parents. If in enemy's House, i.e. House no.7, 10 or 11, one may be asthmatic, but a lover of family; very much attached to father whom he serves well; learned; careless in spending money; must adopt restraint in financial transactions.

3. **Jupiter in Gemini:** Busy in pursuit of knowledge; mentally alert; can be an author; curious to know more and more; a store house of knowledge, especially science. Jupiter hates Mercury and not vice versa, hence sometimes himself responsible for getting less than what he deserves. Nevertheless, intelligent and happiness from relatives and well-to-do family.

4. **Jupiter in Cancer:** The best placement; learned; truthful; charitable; lots of gold and wealth; maintains best relations with all; lovable personality; smiling face; cheerful disposition; courageous in adversity; mother's

blessings; all comforts, vehicles; magnificent house. In fact, the most exalted planet; full of milk of human kindness.

5. **Jupiter in Leo:** Jupiter in friend's sign is exalted. A perfect gentleman; learned; short-tempered because of 'Lion's' influence. A great writer; eminent status; enjoys respect from colleagues and others; noble-hearted; humanitarian; wealthy and eminent sons.

6. **Jupiter in Virgo:** Enjoys life at other's expense; a parasite feeding upon others; gets everything without making any effort; lavish living; shrewd; plays his cards well with a 'smiling face'. Believes in the maxim – "Eat, drink and make merry, who knows the world may end tonight."

7. **Jupiter in Libra:** Asthmatic; a sadhu in previous birth; helper of relatives but never receives their gratitude; will live away from brothers but rich; father of noble, fortunate sons; astrologer; luxurious life; bad investments; a great conversationalist and public speaker; a prolific reader of books.

8. **Jupiter in Scorpio:** Blessings of ancestors; long life; emotional; good financial expert; shrewd; man of determination; courageous; rising fortune. Lots of gold and wealth; will glitter like gold in his career. God's blessings upon him. Proficient in state matters; may earn name and fame, if honest and truthful.

9. **Jupiter in Sagittarius:** Lover of traditions; upholder of family virtues and customs; rich inheritance; intellectual; interested in spiritualism; noble; helpful to all; eminent family; receives blessings from ancestors. An exalted planet in its exalted sign.

10. **Jupiter in Capricorn:** Worst results; though intelligent yet will not get his due, i.e. will get less than what he deserves; loss of wealth; wastage of labour; though noble yet will be deprived of wealth and property. Father may

not leave anything; but self-made rich after 36 years. Disruption in studies; till 36 years of age, his efforts are futile.

11. **Jupiter in Aquarius:** Should be noble, humane and religious-minded for best results; otherwise lonely like a palm tree; timid and cowardly. In this sign Jupiter is almost zero; sisters will be thankless; must not be lustful.

12. **Jupiter in Pisces:** Jupiter is in its own sign, hence noble and good; such a person is tolerant; well-behaved; interested in literature; forgiving nature; good towards enemies even; scholar; humane. The more liberal he is, the more he learns; a lot of expenditure on household articles and good things; honest, truthful and good-doer.

————❖◆❖————

chapter 16

Moon (Chandra)

1. **Moon in Aries:** Emotional; quick-tempered; rich; mother's blessings; pure-hearted like milk; wealthy; long and successful life and service; learned; must respect his mother for best results; money spent on education will not go waste.

2. **Moon in Taurus:** Most exalted; rich parents and in-laws; bringer of best luck; fountain of pure milk; self-made rich; mother's blessings; must be blessed with a son; exalted status. Everything fine in wealth and education.

3. **Moon in Gemini:** Learned; quick-witted and resourceful; best results regarding property, wealth and marital affection; victorious over enemies; good-doer; humane; compassionate, saviour of life; long meaningful life. If adversely aspected by Ketu, results will be worst.

4. **Moon in Cancer:** Fountain of sweet milk and water; benign mother's blessings; complete education. Must respect mother, failing which a loser; emotional; loving; humane; full of tranquillity and peace of mind; bringer of good luck to parents; all comforts and luxuries.

5. **Moon in Leo:** Proud; love for luxurious things; self-indulgent; a great organiser; like a bird of good omen; handsome; polite; intelligent; humane; justice-loving; wealthy; may live abroad; devoted to parents; courageous in adversity; highly qualified, i.e. complete education.

6. **Moon in Virgo:** Shy and retiring; reticent; practical and methodical; learned, i.e. must complete his education; wise; Moon bestows all pleasures in youth but always tense because of Moon in Ketu's / Mercury's sign, i.e. Lunar eclipse.

7. **Moon in Libra:** Courteous; charming behaviour; very rich; incarnation of goddess of wealth. Purity of thoughts and deeds; happy life; mother's patronage; will be respected by all; poet; interested in astrology; all comforts; lots of gold and wealth; must respect the mother for best results. Must complete education before marriage.

8. **Moon in Scorpio:** Worst results on mind and heart; highly emotional and depressed. If Moon in Taurus is exalted, it is most malefic in Scorpio. Afflicted with epilepsy; diseases of the heart; weak heart; insanity; but bringer of good luck; will definitely be blessed with a son; long life; must not be lustful.

9. **Moon in Sagittarius:** Rich inheritance; polite, humane; like a beautiful pearl; incarnation of 'Moon', i.e. noble; good-doer; full of milk of human kindness; may travel abroad; influential leader respected by all; ocean of knowledge; life full of comforts and luxuries; best luck with the blessings of parents.

10. **Moon in Capricorn:** Moon in this sign is weak like sour and bitter milk; an unsuccessful physician but a great surgeon; in-laws and property will be destroyed; may earn bad name; enmity with mother; obstacles in education but long life.

11. **Moon in Aquarius:** Most malefic; Moon is reduced to zero in this sign. Life full of storms and whirlpools; weak in body; wild temperament; eccentric; moody; will however receive complete education; even if illiterate such a person is shrewd, subtle and intelligent; but most erratic and wild behaviour.

12. Moon in Pisces: Idealistic; dreamer – always dreaming of the glorious past; highly sensitive; interested in occult; may even possess psychic powers; must control his pro-active sensibilities and highly charged imagination; face like that of white cat; prone to flattery. Wife – source of strength in adversity; inherited property may be destroyed but will enjoy self-acquired wealth and property. Best results regarding education for self and children.

Venus (Shukra)

1. **Venus in Aries:** No discrimination of caste and creed in matters of love; but good for service, wealth and monetary benefits; undependable; like a moth hovering over other women; all family members will get advantage; leader in the family; bad health of spouse; romantic temperament; impulsive and emotional in matters of love; excessive sex may cause ruin.

2. **Venus in Taurus:** Most exalted, being in its own sign; all comforts – wealth, marital happiness, domestic peace. Victory over enemies; wooed by many beautiful women; faithful; refined and graceful behaviour; but passionate and sensual – the characteristics of Venus – the goddess of love and beauty; lover of luxuries with extravagant tastes; exalted status. Venus bestows all her charms upon the native.

3. **Venus in Gemini:** Loyal and devoted wife; best results; charitable disposition (amicable disposition); polite and sociable. In adversity, she inspires him and acts like a bold man. Must not cheat his wife.

4. **Venus in Cancer:** Travels on land will bring best results; clash between wife and mother-in-law after about four years as Moon is hostile to Venus and not vice versa. In the beginning all comforts, luxuries and wealth; prone to changing moods, like the waxing and waning of Moon. Sensitive and romantic, imbibing the traits of both Venus and Moon.

5. **Venus in Leo:** Affectionate; deeply attached to family; cheerful; may earn a lot; easily attracted to the opposite sex. If of good conduct, life is fine; if lustful, then worst results.

6. **Venus in Virgo:** Most malefic; carpet knight; flatterer of women; may suffer from skin ailments; insulting attitude towards relations; domestic peace is destroyed; may do foolish acts but protected by Nature; may be even sexually weak; sex-ridden.

7. **Venus in Libra:** Best placement, as Venus is in her own exalted sign; if alone, it is the most exalted – domestic happiness; wealthy; noble and loyal wife; a very happy couple indeed; interested in fine arts, poetry, music, love of all good things including beautiful women.

8. **Venus in Scorpio:** Malefic; short-tempered; always angry; ill-fated; sickly; haughty spouse; emotional intensity and over indulgence in sex may cause ruin; must not marry before 25th year (the age of Venus).

9. **Venus in Sagittarius:** Resourceful; wise; administrator; though rich yet will have to work hard for livelihood; darling of the society; source of inspiration to others; achieves fame and name through his own efforts.

10. **Venus in Capricorn:** Venus is Saturn's friend. If Saturn is exalted, Venus automatically confers best results regarding wealth, domestic happiness, luxury of conveyance; power. Sometimes he marries in a rich status family. If of lustful conduct and unfaithful to wife, he is ruined. Such a person is lover of women in youth but a noble preacher in old age – case of sinner in youth turning preacher in old age.

11. **Venus in Aquarius:** Beautiful wife; rich man; outwardly a simpleton, but very clever and subtle like a snake. Being in Saturn's sign, it confers a lot of wealth; irreligious; lover of fairer sex; rebellious and lover of

good things of life; given to eccentric and strange mode of dress.

12. **Venus in Pisces:** Most exalted; wife confers all pleasures – sexual and domestic. Best luck after marriage; exalted status; supporter of family; full of enthusiasm; poet; fond of music and all beautiful and fine things of life; romantic and idealistic; full of compassion and milk of human kindness. In fact, best placement in the Birth chart.

———————❖◆❖———————

CHAPTER 18

Mars (Mangal)

1. **Mars in Aries:** Mars in its own exalted sign makes the person brave like a tiger; army or police officer; justice-loving; like a sword in its sheath; leader; trustful, fair and just; resourceful; eminent status; bureaucrat; good government job; independent and headstrong; a great organiser; full of zeal and zest.

2. **Mars in Taurus:** Quarrelsome; jealous; possessive; tactless; undiplomatic; highly sexed; may destroy his own property; opposition to and from his brothers; but brave enough to ward off attacks by enemies; full of determination and fortitude in adversity.

3. **Mars in Gemini:** Restlessness, mental agility, determination, justice-loving, sarcastic wit are the hallmarks of "Mars in Gemini". Good for others but bad for self in respect of money and peace; chest problem; like a tiger in the zoo.

4. **Mars in Cancer:** Most malefic; full of fire; diabolic tendencies; destroyer of happiness and wealth; worst placement, if not aspected by Sun, Moon or Jupiter; disease of stomach, intestines, uterus and womb; burn or wound mark.

5. **Mars in Leo:** Brave like a lion; of firm opinions, passionate; qualities of leadership; competent and

efficient; ancestor of rich progeny; scholarly; learned; very rich; helpful to all.

6. **Mars in Virgo:** A contented saint or dervish; all pleasure from friends and spouse; must earn more than brothers; noble hearted; sweet in speech; exalted position; popular among officers, colleagues and subordinates, etc.; devoted to parents. A good organiser of work force; precise in all details and man of perseverance and resolution.

7. **Mars in Libra:** Supporter of family; very rich; lots of property; reliable; competent adviser; jolly; just; good status. Marriage is more for social companionship than physical satisfaction; though sexually strong.

8. **Mars in Scorpio:** Industrious; courageous; powerful personality; domineering; ruthless towards enemies, believes in the maxim – "Tit for Tat". Possessive and jealous in romantic relationships; extreme temperament; but a death trap; noose of death around the neck; accident prone; wound and burn marks on the body. Expert in military affairs; intelligent but fear of death till 28 years. May be ring leader of shady characters, but still leads a life of luxury; bad for marital happiness.

9. **Mars in Sagittarius:** Mars in this sign confers all wealth, comforts and happiness; administrator; ancestral wealth and greatness; precious ruby for family. Bringer of good luck to parents and self; lover of traditions; religious-minded; spiritualist in the fag end of life; full of strong, moral courage and convictions. A good placement indeed.

10. **Mars in Capricorn:** Most exalted; royal and eminent status; life full of honey and sweetness; bold like a tiger; rich; lots of property; ambitious; decisive; independent in thinking. Head of an organisation, army or civil services; very famous; domestic happiness; good health. A renowned and powerful leader, provided it should be alone and not aspected by enemy planet.

11. **Mars in Aquarius:** Exalted; life sweet like honey; noble, rich; king-like status at the age of 28 years; all comforts and luxuries; independent thinking; very intelligent; unconventional in his approach to problems.

12. **Mars in Pisces:** Unhappy married life; bad eyesight; believer in occult; emotional; brooding nature; unnecessary and foolish expenditure; diseased; lack of confidence.

❖◆❖

Mercury (Budh)

1. **Mercury in Aries:** Though selfish, yet such a person achieves honour, fame and exalted status; will never lose wealth; mercurial temperament; hence unreliable but clever; pleasing to fair sex and proficient; impulsive and hasty in his decisions; outspoken.

2. **Mercury in Taurus:** Man of letters; sweet-tongued; best fate; lucky but selfish; writer; public speaker; victorious; witty; self-made rich; inflexible in his views; cheerful; pleasure-seeker; long-lived.

3. **Mercury in Gemini:** Good for self but bad for others; good reasoning power; inquisitive; eloquent; fickle like a eunuch; lack of emotional warmth but well versed in scriptures.

4. **Mercury in Cancer:** Most exalted; man of letters; like a philosopher's stone turning baser metal into gold; good for self and wife; but restless; precious diamond of the family; very rich; indeed an exalted sign, if alone.

5. **Mercury in Leo:** Learned; scholarly; an astrologer; truthful; wealthy; but a little arrogant and peevish; good speaker and organiser.

6. **Mercury in Virgo:** Exalted being in its own sign; rich; liberal; successful and prosperous in business; versatile and intelligent; famous writer or speaker or poet; master of lands; victory over opponents. Must be honest and not greedy, if doctor; logical in reasoning.

7. **Mercury in Libra:** Precious diamond for the family; successful businessman; victory in all court cases; learned; forceful writer; like a philosopher's stone helping and enriching others, but rich himself too. Peaceful and harmonious life; creative and artistic; may be interested in modelling and fine arts.

8. **Mercury in Scorpio:** Most malefic; ill-fated; notorious; sex-ridden; addicted to vices; loser of wealth; an infectious leper; a fading flower; foul-mouthed; sharp tongue; sarcastic and critical; subtle and shy; disease of mouth, teeth and tongue. White ant eating up the house; financial losses.

9. **Mercury in Sagittarius:** Being in enemy sign, it is malefic; such a person is ill-fated, like a bat hanging upside down; helper of family member; unreliable like a shameless maid; but sincere, versatile and humane; even a learned writer.

10. **Mercury in Capricorn:** It is a friendly sign, hence comfortable life but a sycophant, selfish, subtle and cunning like a snake; ambitious, shrewd, materialistic but narrow-minded. Lacking sense of humour. If Saturn is malefic, everything goes awry and wrong. Addiction to drug and wine will ruin him. Malefic Saturn's effect is visible on his psyche, i.e. he is wicked and sly like a stinging snake.

11. **Mercury in Aquarius:** Mercury's effect will depend on Jupiter – good or bad; wealth and property after 34th year, i.e. after Mercury's life period; like a diamond; but ill-omened like an owl; accursed; foolish; worst results till 34th year. Such a person is unemotional but can see through enemy's sinister schemes; interested in occult and astrology.

12. **Mercury in Pisces:** If alone, it is the most devastating and malefic; comfortable long life, but sleepless nights;

day dreamers; over sensitive and artistic, hence full of unfettered imagination; self-respecting but deceiver at heart; such a person is like a mad dog; wavering nature; unreliable; sharp-tongued; rash; bad for speculations; may face humiliation, ignominy and loss of wealth, etc. Especially Mercury in Pisces alone in House no. 12 is the worst in the Birth chart.

Saturn (Shani)

1. **Saturn in Aries:** Most malefic; worst fate; thankless wretch; wicked and sinful; stubborn and obstinate; lazy; slothful. Even if born to rich parents, worst fate awaits him; long life; but poor. If Saturn and Venus are both in Aries and in 1st House, worst fate; accursed; everything will be auctioned; disruption in studies; liar; dishonest; cheat; thief; quarrelsome. If Mars is in Capricorn, Saturn in Aries will no longer be malefic; being the sign (Raashi) of the deadliest foe, such a person receives no royal favours; no name and fame; no sympathy and friendship; discontented; writhing and twisting like a wounded snake.

2. **Saturn in Taurus:** In friend's sign, it is quite benefic; healthy; outwardly simpleton, but shrewd and wise; intelligent; efficient adviser; kind, merciful; humane; just and fair; lots of landed property; leader among men; good status and comfortable living; reliable, methodical; competent; may be untrustworthy and unreliable because of the characteristics of snake and Venus.

3. **Saturn in Gemini:** Malefic; hypocrite; pretends to be virtuous and noble, whereas he is a snake up the sleeve. "Man may smile and smile, yet be a villain." Oversexed; not liked by people; may lose wealth; relatives may cause harm; lacks in emotional warmth and sense of humour; austere. If person is not addicted to drugs then long and comfortable life.

4. **Saturn in Cancer:** May be deprived of mother's love in childhood, but due to his own efforts can reach the top. Saturn will never exercise bad effect; may deal in medicines and take after father's profession; emotionally sensitive. If addicted to drugs, may suffer from problems in the eyes.

5. **Saturn in Leo:** Saturn is Sun's greatest enemy, hence the most malefic; unfortunate; thief or cheat having Satanic tendencies; well read-but poor; life full of troubles; bad health; involved in litigation; case of a snake feeding upon its children; insipid and ordinary life; unreliable; stubborn; strong willed; inflexible in his attitude.

6. **Saturn in Virgo:** Though proficient in his field of action, yet a rank opportunist; a severe critic; shrewd; practical; lacking emotional warmth; no sense of humour. Retrograde; it hurts even Venus in Taurus, its own friend; will be blessed with son; wealthy, intelligent and wise.

7. **Saturn in Libra:** Most auspicious and exalted; great organiser; best marital life; doctor or engineer or administrator, if Mars is exalted. Can be competent negotiator or mediator or arbitrator. Earns name, wealth and fame through his own efforts; very rich; noble and kind hearted; long life; may travel a lot; best placement indeed.

8. **Saturn in Scorpio:** Short-tempered; over-sexed; man of extreme temperament; always full of anger; violent; hard task master, hence opposed by colleagues and subordinates; Judges others from his own yardstick; snake whether alive or dead in its burrow causes scare.

9. **Saturn in Sagittarius:** Most exalted and auspicious; rich; compassionate; owner of land and houses; comfortable life; must be generous and large-hearted for better effect; like a costly black and seasoned wood; best fate; academically ambitious; intellectual; famous authority in his profession; leader among compatriots and colleagues.

[81]

10. **Saturn in Capricorn:** Exalted, being in its own sign; successful in all ventures; exalted status; authoritative; exercises lot of influence and power over others; rich; lots of property; all comforts and pleasures; but deceitful; should be bold and strict, otherwise will be destroyed if weak and humble.

11. **Saturn in Aquarius:** Architect of one's own fate; most exalted, as it is in its own sign; practical; single track mind; full of concentration in job and work; puts all his energies in intellectual pursuits; industrious; may build houses and earn wealth; will be destroyed if addicted to wine.

12. **Saturn in Pisces:** Imaginative; artistic; full of the milk of human kindness; introvert and shy in nature; very rich; comfortable life; full of fortitude during bad times; may be baldheaded after 36 years of age and that is the sign of richness. Saturn, i.e. benefic snake, protects the man, instead of stinging him; exalted status and exalted business, being in Jupiter's sign.

————————❖◆❖————————

CHAPTER

21

Rahu

1. **Rahu in Aries:** May see many ups and downs; sometimes very rich and sometimes worst fate; himself responsible for his misfortunes. Solar eclipse on one side, but all brightness on the other side, i.e. may lose one job, the other may be readily available; bitter tongue; anger; illness; baseless superstitions.

2. **Rahu in Taurus:** Rahu is enemy of Venus, hence marital discord; wealthy but insecure; short-tempered; bitter tongue; bad fate; may be involved in criminal cases or frauds for no fault of his; rise and fall; exalted status. If noble, good results.

3. **Rahu in Gemini:** Most exalted; strong-willed and arrogant; long life of pleasures and comforts; very rich and powerful; tiger-like voice; bold and fearless; enemies will tremble; owner of landed property; will rise to great heights; king-like status.

4. **Rahu in Cancer:** Noble and pious like a yogi; broad-minded but unlucky with friends who may cheat him; rich; but full of tension, being in Moon's sign.

5. **Rahu in Leo:** In enemy's sign it wreaks havoc; haughty; notorious; health problems; may be witty and intellectual but will not rise till Rahu's period; problem in birth of son. After Rahu's period, will rise very high in life; will be very rich with all luxuries.

6. **Rahu in Virgo:** Most exalted; destroyer of enemies; eminent status; elephant at his beck and call; conferring all wealth, power, status and luxuries; Rahu acts as a shield and protects the man from calamities; very intelligent; self-respecting and proud. The best placement indeed.

7. **Rahu in Libra:** Worst; disturbed family life; though rich, yet cruel and insensitive to other's feelings. Early marriage may result in wife's death or separation; hard task master; proficient in his work; high status; victory over enemies; wife may be physically weak; no happiness from children, though occupying good jobs; others may enjoy his wealth. If lustful, worst results.

8. **Rahu in Scorpio:** Being in enemy's sign and House of death, Rahu becomes most malefic. Man is weak, poor, sickly and wicked; ups and downs in life. If dishonest and corrupt, loss of wealth; meaningless struggles, quarrels, chatter; unnecessary expenditure. Blows the trumpet of death, i.e. lays death trap. Must not lose courage in adversity and must be of good character.

9. **Rahu in Sagittarius:** Malefic; Solar eclipse; dishonest psychiatrist; suffers a lot since early age; may be adopted by someone; may even cheat his friends and spouse; bad for career and business; dishonesty will ruin him. Unfavourable speech; dark fate. Being in Jupiter's sign, fate will be later on revived, as Jupiter and Rahu are of equal strength. Because of Jupiter's effect, such a person may become leader of men and earn a lot.

10. **Rahu in Capricorn:** Being in a friendly sign, Rahu confers all honour, power, wealth, authority like a "Sapphire" (Mani) on snake's head; fearless; helpful to others, but dishonest too; good for parents; rich and bold; exalted status; will earn a lot through business and industry; rise after marriage. If Saturn is weak in the Birth chart, he may suffer financially and may lose property as well, through jealousy and meanness – the attributes of a stinging snake.

11. **Rahu in Aquarius:** Long life; wealthy through fraudulent and corrupt practices; influential though reticent; bad for father's life, but will not financially suffer as long as father is alive; parents may suffer losses after his birth; till then very comfortable position.

12. **Rahu in Pisces:** Rahu in its own sign is malefic and weak; a lot of unnecessary expenditure; in evil deeds; secretive; may live abroad; proficient in his work; stifling smoke; day-dreamer; involvement in criminal cases, litigation; full of ugly thoughts; clashes with all. Jupiter's or Saturn's results may be exalted, but Rahu's effect is the worst, like a mad elephant trampling over its own master; hard-working but sleepless nights; may earn bad name.

———————❖◆❖———————

CHAPTER 22

Ketu

1. **Ketu in Aries:** In enemy's sign, it gives bad results; full of unnecessary worries and fears; unhappy; tale carrier but a good orator; a linguist; may suffer from windy troubles; worried about children and job, but will have a son and another job, i.e. misplaced worries; will serve well father as well as teacher.

2. **Ketu in Taurus:** Traveller; a good talker; noble; sadhu; unhappy with relatives; but prosperous administrator; generous and liberal; may be opposed by mother, but the darling of wife.

3. **Ketu in Gemini:** Contented sadhu; brave; wealthy but restless for brothers; may live away from relatives; good-doer; forgets the harm done to him but is grateful to the benefactor; may even be opposed by brothers; even children will not give him happiness and solace; may live abroad and earn a lot.

4. **Ketu in Cancer:** Ketu in the sign of its deadliest foe, i.e. Moon is the most malefic, but noble, pious, wise and resourceful; a groaning or a complaining dog, i.e. may lose lands, property and all comforts, loss of wealth, full of imaginary worries and wild thoughts. May live away from home; bad for mother; hard-working but always restless and under tension; complete Lunar eclipse, i.e. mind is perturbed and health is lost.

5. **Ketu in Leo:** Makes a person timid and short-tempered; Sun's effect becomes dim; full of evil thoughts. Handsome, but if lustful, he becomes a withered flower. If of good character, will be blessed with sons and good status. If Jupiter is weak, son may suffer from allergies and respiratory troubles; devoted to father.

6. **Ketu in Virgo:** Most malefic; complete Lunar eclipse; shrewd and intelligent; sees through the enemy's diabolical schemes. If Jupiter is exalted in the Birth chart, everything is fine – long life, good sons, wealthy; may visit foreign lands; but unreliable and cowardly who loses his confidence, as Ketu is weak in its own sign, being Mercury's enemy.

7. **Ketu in Libra:** Tiger-like dog; lots of wealth; lovable character; second dutiful son; victory over enemies; enemies will be doomed; but should not be an egoist; must keep his word, failing which he will be a loser. If bitter and sharp-tongued, unhappy family life.

8. **Ketu in Scorpio:** Short-lived; wound marks with weapons; or stinging bite from scorpion; may have premonition of death; like a groaning dog mourning the losses. Must not be of loose character; he will then invite his own doom in matters of health, family life and wife's health.

9. **Ketu in Sagittarius:** Exalted; bringer of good luck for parents; may live abroad; bold like a tiger and faithful like a dog; best adviser; dutiful sons; advantage in travels; bad for mother; self-made rich.

10. **Ketu in Capricorn:** Saturn's position – good or bad – decides Ketu's fate; rich but lustful; all luxuries at his feet; hard-working; brave and a leader. It is the lust for sex with other women that will destroy him; must be of good character and everything will be fine and rosy.

11. **Ketu in Aquarius:** Meagre earnings; no fame; no reward for his merit; jackal-like dog; learned and intelligent; less of landed property, but earnings will increase after

36 years. In a girl's horoscope, it will be just the reverse, i.e. a good placement; bad for mother. If Saturn is in man's horoscope, wife may lose son in the womb.

12. **Ketu in Pisces:** Exalted; will earn from travels and lands; rich and healthy sons; very rich; may inherit property; life full of comforts and luxuries, prestige; devoted to parents, helpful to others but unhappy with brothers and in-laws; sons and brothers will occupy good position in service.

❖◆❖

CHAPTER 23

How to Read a Birth Chart

While examining a Birth chart, please do not be in a hurry to make predictions simply on the basis of a single planet. Birth chart should be read carefully in all aspects, their placement in their own Signs (Raashis) or Houses, their friendly or Enemy Signs and Houses, should be considered while giving your opinion. It is possible that the planet may be exalted but if it is aspected by a powerful enemy, it loses its lustre and does not give the same effect.

Results of Exalted Planets:

(a) **Exalted Sun** in its own House and Raashi gives the best results, i.e. power, wealth, respect, name and fame, glory, all luxuries and comforts; dominance over others. Such a person will shine like the Sun on the firmament of life; very famous indeed.

(b) **Exalted Moon** in its own House and Raashi confers wealth, honour, fame, though slippery and unsteady, gives all luxuries and pleasures of marital life.

(c) **Exalted Jupiter** in its own House and Raashi confers knowledge, nobility, generosity, etc. Such a man is wise, learned, well versed in morals; reliable; linguist; a good adviser.

(d) **Exalted Mars** in its own House and Raashi confers all authority, power, position, exalted status in police or army or some famous organisation. Such a person never fails in his duty; rich, with a large number of servants and subordinates.

(e) **Exalted Mercury** in its own House and Raashi makes a man learned; eminent; writer or poet, doctor, editor, mathematician, businessman; auditor; accountant; honoured by society for his erudition and scholarship; jovial in disposition.

(f) **Exalted Venus** in its own House and Raashi – such a person is a great lover of music, poetry, dance, beautiful women; full of zest for sexual life; life of luxury in the company of women who court and help him. Very lucky; happy domestic life; rise after marriage.

(g) **Exalted Saturn** in its own House and Raashi – such a person is a rich landowner; leader of men; gets wealth from unexpected quarters; winner of lottery; may earn through speculations and investments; treasurer.

(h) **Exalted Rahu** in its own exalted House and Raashi – such a man achieves eminence, power, authority and wealth through fraudulent means and by browbeating others; sex-ridden; elephant that raises the man to the skies and makes him rich.

(i) **Exalted Ketu** in its own exalted House and Raashi – such a man is bringer of good luck to parents, bold like a pig and faithful like a dog; lives abroad; eminent status; rich; generous and stingy both; sex-ridden; leader or captain of a team.

(j) **Exalted Planets** in friend's Houses and in their own Raashis also give beneficial results, but not as exalted as the ones enumerated above.

Planets in friend's Houses and Raashis are also benefic and confer good results.

Exalted planets in their own Raashi, but in Inimical Houses are partially good and partially bad.

Debilitating or Inauspicious Planets

(a) **Sun in Debilitation:** In enemy's House and enemy's Sign (Raashi) gives the worst results; such a man is jealous, always ready to obey others; sinful and a mean rival; faces humiliation; ignominy; is mocked by all and butt of ridicule.

(b) **Moon in Debilitation:** In enemy's House and Sign gives the worst results; insane; epileptic; undependable; mean spy; sickly; destroyer of wealth; given to fits and swoons; always worried; tense and depressed; suffers because of mother.

(c) **Jupiter in Debilitation:** In enemy's House and Sign – poor sadhu; though learned like Sudama (a poor friend of Lord Krishna); ignoble; given to self-praise; little prospects in life; faces many ups and downs; receives bad publicity though innocent.

(d) **Mars in Debilitation:** In enemy's House and Sign – an ungrateful wretch; destroyer of wealth and property; a doubting Thomas; thief; terrorist; lustful; malicious in speech and deeds; instigator of riots; wicked; full of venom, hatred and ill-will.

(e) **Venus in Debilitation:** In enemy's House and Sign – lustful; wicked; lover of women; illicit relations with women of loose morals; a physical wreck; may suffer from diseases; a senile and wretched domestic life.

(f) **Mercury in Debilitation:** In enemy's House and Sign – an insipid and ordinary life; may run away from home; destroyer of everything; reviled and mocked by all. Incoherent talker; talks a lot, but all meaningless; flatterer, sycophant; useless and mean knowledge.

(g) **Saturn in Debilitation:** In enemy's House and Sign – a drunkard; a stinging snake up the sleeves; full of mean and bad thoughts; subtle and vile conspirator; a poor labourer; illiterate; may commit foul and dirty acts; always unhappy; a blind horoscope; lustful and given to bad ways of life.

(h) **Rahu in Debilitation:** In enemy's House and Sign – a litigant; involved in criminal cases; earns by cheating and looting others; but still under debt; hand to mouth living; unnecessary expenditure; but achieves his goal by crushing others; a polluted and notorious mind full of malice; a perverted genius; misdirected intellect.

(i) **Ketu in Debilitation:** Ketu is Rahu's serf and slave. It acts according to its master's dictates; hence as mean and vile as Rahu; a roguish bad son; a complaining dog. Inauspicious for the family; a son who brings bad name to parents.

———————❖◆❖———————

CHAPTER 25

Important Lessons

You must have read of the phrase "Fools rush in, where angels fear to tread". Don't be rash and in a hurry. Read the Birth chart in its entirety. For instance, when you find Saturn in Aries (1) in House no. 1 (Lagna or Ascendant), do not behave like an oracle and pronounce worst results for such a person. No please. Look at the other houses such as House no. 10 – if you find Mars in it, in Capricorn (10), then announce at once that Saturn is no longer malefic; as it is fully aspected by Mars, the real Lord of this House and Sign. Isn't it a case of "strange bedfellows"? Let me elucidate it still further: suppose both of us are deadly foes. If you occupy my House and I yours, both of us will not have the guts to harm each other. It will then be a case of "Live and let live" or else "Perish together". Then what is the best solution? Let us then be good to each other. As in politics, so is the case with planets. To further their own interests, they shake hands with enemies even. Deadly foes now become friends in order to protect their own interests.

Let me cite another instance. Suppose Moon is in Taurus in House no. 2, but it is afflicted by Saturn from House no. 6 or 8. In that case Moon is destroyed and it loses its sheen and exalted placement. Thus all the aspects by friends and enemies must be taken into consideration before arriving at some conclusion.

Two, Three or More Planets:
The following facts may be considered while making predictions about two or three or more planets in a Birth chart.

1. They usually give their own individual effect; but often they blend into each other. If friendly, the results are benefic and if opposed to each other, results may not be good; but not necessarily bad.

2. Enemy planets give up their opposition.

3. Female planets in conjunction with male planets confer good results.

Some Exalted Examples:

1. **Sun - Jupiter:** Most exalted; kingly status; royal heritage and wealth.

2. **Sun - Mars:** Rich landlord; administrator; royal wealth and inheritance.

3. **Jupiter - Mars:** Very wealthy.

4. **Jupiter - Venus:** Wealth for outward appearance.

5. **Jupiter - Moon:** Lots of wealth and gold; may receive legacy from parents.

6. **Jupiter - Saturn:** Lots of wealth after marriage in a rich family.

7. **Moon - Mars:** Lots of wealth, if in House no.3. Rich but greedy if in House no. 10 or 11.

8. **Moon - Saturn:** Lots of wealth, if with Jupiter; or in Jupiter's permanent House viz. 2, 5, 9, 12; otherwise bad for health and wealth.

9. **Mars - Venus:** Though rich, yet wealth is controlled by wife.

Some Malefic Examples:

1. **Sun - Rahu:** Complete Solar eclipse; self-created problems in career; unnecessary expenditure; problems in health; prone to allergy.

2. **Sun - Saturn:** Bad domestic life; unreliable person; weak body; Saturn blackens Sun's face and energy.

3. **Moon - Ketu:** Complete Lunar eclipse; prone to allergy; always depressed and under tension.

4. **Moon - Venus:** Clash of ego between the mother-in-law and daughter-in-law four years after marriage.

5. **Venus - Rahu:** Unhappy married life; problems in birth of a son; bad health of spouse; may suffer from piles.

6. **Mars - Ketu (malefic):** Tremors in hand and feet; palsy, i.e. shaking of head.

Wicked Planets and their Deadly Aspects:

Saturn, Rahu, Ketu are devils incarnate. Saturn is the chief of sinners and Rahu and Ketu are its agents.

If they aspect enemy planet or planets, all the enemies will be destroyed, i.e. they give worst effect. Even if a friend is associated with enemy planet or planets, he also comes in the firing range of these rogues, i.e. he is also destroyed during the indiscriminate firing. There is a also a catch here: though Rahu is Saturn's agent to accomplish the former's evil designs; yet if Saturn aspects Rahu, Rahu gives the worst results but if Rahu aspects Saturn, the results are the best.

Kendra and other Houses:

1. Four Kendras, i.e. House no. 1, 4, 7 and 10 are the most important. If they are vacant, it clearly indicates that one has to strive for one's fate.

2. Man's fate then depends upon House No. 3, 5, 9 and 11. House no. 3 refers to brothers; House no. 5 to children; House no. 9 to ancestral wealth and House no. 11 to one's own efforts to carve out his own destiny.

3. Suppose the above Houses are also vacant, search for the planet of Destiny in House no. 2, 6, 8 and 12. This is the last resort.

❖◆❖

Mahadasha Calculation

In the previous chapters, I have discussed in detail the fundamentals of Astrology, Houses, Planets in their Exalted or Debilitated Signs (Raashis), and Aspects to acquaint the reader of the finest nuances of this great science of divination. Now let me come to the main point, i.e. computation of Mahadasha (Main period), Antardasha (Sub-period) and Pratyantar dasha (Sub-sub-period). There are obviously two schools of thoughts regarding the full cycle of man's life. North Indian astrologers take man's total life of longevity as 120 years and divide the cycle of planets accordingly. This is called "Vimshottari cycle of life". The South Indian astrologers calculate total life-span as of 108 years and divide the cycle of planets accordingly. It is called "Ashtottari cycle of life". The total spans of life of planets in both the systems are different. Let me discuss both the systems for the convenience of the readers.

Vimshottari System of Mahadasha:

1. Total longevity of life = 120 years

2. Life-span of Planets:

    (a)   Sun — 6 years

    (b)   Moon — 10 years

    (c)   Mars — 7 years

    (d)   Rahu — 18 years

    (e)   Jupiter — 16 years

    (f)   Saturn — 19 years

(g)   Mercury — 17 years

(h)   Ketu — 7 years

(i)   Venus — 20 years

Total life cycle = 120 years

The planets function in the above order.

I. Dasha at the time of Birth: Dasha is calculated from the positioning of Moon in a particular "Nakshatra" or "Constellation" or "Lunar mansion" at the time of birth. Zodiac is divided into 27 Nakshatras, each extending to 13 degress and 20 minutes of arc of 800'. The moon may occupy any degree or minute in the ruling Nakshatra at birth. The order in which the Dasha periods of planets are reckoned is as under:

Constellation			Planet	Duration
Ashwani	Magha	Mool	Ketu	7 years
Bharni	P.Phalguni	P. Shada	Venus	20 years
Kritika	U.Phalguni	U. Shada	Sun	6 years
Rohini	Hastha	Shravana	Moon	10 years
Mrigshira	Chitra	Dhanishta	Mars	7 years
Ardra	Swati	Shatbhisha	Rahu	18 years
Punarvasu	Vishakha	P. Bhadra	Jupiter	16 years
Pushya	Anuradha	U. Bhadra	Saturn	19 years
Ashlesha	Jyeshtha	Revati	Mercury	17 years

The duration of the initial Mahadasha is reckoned from the distance traversed by Moon at the time of birth. **Example:** Suppose a person is born in Ashwani Nakshatra. It means Ketu was the Lord of Mahadasha ruling at birth. Thus first Mahadasha will be of 7 years of Ketu; followed by Venus (20 years); Sun (6 years); Moon (6 years) and so on and so forth. Further, suppose child is born with the Moon in the middle of 'Ardra Nakshatra', it means that the Lord of 'Ardra', i.e. '**Rahu**' has already covered half of its Dasha period, i.e. 9 years; hence its period of Mahadasha may be reduced by 9 years; thereafter, Jupiter (16 years); Saturn (19 years) and so on and so forth.

[97]

All the 9 planets rule over the constellations (Nakshatras) in three cycles. Now divide the number of Nakshatras between the **Birth Nakshatras** and **Kritika (no.3 constellation)** by 9. The remainder is the commencement of the Mahadasha of a planet in the following order: Sun, Moon, Mars, Rahu, Jupiter, Mercury, Ketu and Venus.

Planet	Nakshatra's Number	Years of Mahadasha
1. Sun	3, 12, 21	6 years
2. Moon	4, 13, 22	10 years
3. Mars	5, 14, 23	7 years
4. Rahu	6, 15, 24	18 years
5. Jupiter	7, 16, 25	16 years
6. Saturn	8, 17, 26	19 years
7. Mercury	9, 18, 27	17 years
8. Ketu	10, 19, 1	7 years
9. Venus	11, 20, 2	20 years

Note:

(a) 3 means Kritika, 12 denotes Uttar Phalguni and 21 refers to Uttar Shada. Please refer to chart of 27 Nakshatras (constellation) in the previous pages.

(b) Starting from Kritika (no.3 of constellation) add 9 and 9; it comes to 3, 12, 21 (nos. of constellations). These Nakshatras refer to Sun's period; Next comes Moon – 4+9+9, i.e. 4, 13, 22 (nos. of constellations). Then comes Mars – 5+9+9, i.e. 5, 14, 23 (nos. of constellations) and so on and so forth. It may be noted that sidereal Zodiac starts from 0° Ashwani which has been numbered 1 in the list.

II. Antardasha (sub-period): Every planet during its Mahadasha period has its sub-periods as well. For example, in the Mahadasha of Moon – the first Antardasha (sub-period) will be that of Moon, followed by those of Mars, Rahu, Jupiter, Saturn, Mercury, Ketu and Venus in that order.

III. How to compute Antardasha (sub-period): The best method of calculating the sub-period of another planet in the Mahadasha of a particular planet is as follows:

$$\frac{\text{(Mahadasha years of a planet} \times \text{Mahadasha of planet for sub-period)}}{40}$$

Suppose we want to find out the sub-period of Rahu in Moon's Mahadasha, let us work it out as under:

1st Method: 18 × 10 = 180.

First two digits will indicate months; the third digit may be multiplied by 3 to calculate days. Thus sub-period of Rahu in Moon's Mahadasha is 18 months and zero days, i.e.

Year	Month	Day
1	6	0

2nd Method: (18 × 10) / 10 = 180 / 10 = 18 months

IV. How to find out the Pratyantar Dasha (sub-sub-period) in the main Dasha:

1st Method: Suppose we want to calculate the Pratyantar Dasha (sub-sub-period) of Jupiter in the Antardasha (sub-period) of Rahu and main Dasha of Moon: Calculate it with the following method:

$$\frac{(\text{Jupiter's period} \times \text{Rahu's period} \times \text{Moon's period})}{40}$$

$$= (16 \times 18 \times 10) / 40 = 72 \text{ days}$$

2nd Method: For calculating Antardasha (sub-period) method:

Coefficient of Mahadasha Lord = *Mahadasha years × 3 days

*(Sun's coefficient is 6 × 3 = 18 days; Moon's coefficient is 10 × 3 = 30 days; Mars' coefficient is 7 × 3 = 21 days; Rahu's coefficient is 18 × 3 = 54 days, and so on and so forth)

Planet	Days
Sun	6 × 3 = 18 days
Moon	10 × 3 = 30 days
Mars	7 × 3 = 21 days
Rahu	18 × 3 = 54 days
Jupiter	16 × 3 = 48 days
Saturn	19 × 3 = 57 days
Mercury	17 × 3 = 51 days
Ketu	7 × 3 = 21 days
Venus	20 × 3 = 60 days

Suppose we want to find out Saturn's Antardasha in Moon Dasha then,

10 × 57 = 570 days = 19 months

Or

Jupiter's Antardasha in Jupiter:

16 × 48 = 768 days, i.e. 25 months + 6 days

Computerised Birth charts give detailed information, but an astrologer must have knowledge of all these methods. One can work them out at once by remembering the above formulae. For the convenience of readers, chart showing Mahadasha, Antardasha and Pratyantar dasha is appended.

V. Ashtottari Dasha System:

This system is prevalent in South India, where the wheel of life is fixed at 108 years and the planets are allotted the following span of years:

Planet	Duration
Sun	6 years
Moon	15 years
Mars	8 years
Mercury	17 years
Saturn	10 years
Jupiter	19 years
Rahu	12 years
Venus	21 years
Total	**108 years**

Format for Birth Chart in South India:

12	1 (Aries)	2	3
11			4
10			5
9	8	7	6

Birth Chart

12 (Sun, Venus)	1 (Rahu)	2 (Jupiter)	3
11 (Mars, Mercury)			4
10			5
9 (Saturn)	8 (Ascendant, Lagna)	7 (Ketu, Moon)	6

Conversion of this Birth Chart into North Indian Pattern:

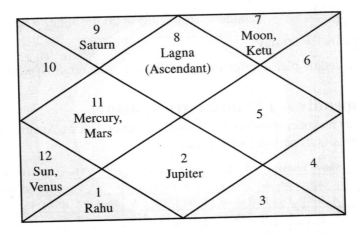

In the computerised horoscopes, all these details are available. However, for the convenience of the readers, I have calculated in the enclosed appendix the Mahadashas and Antardashas of various planets and their allotted span of life in the Ashtottari system.

How to determine Antardasha in Ashtottari System:

Suppose we want to calculate the Antardasha of Jupiter in the Mahadasha of Moon. We adopt the following formula:

Example no. 1:

$$\frac{15(\text{Moon's Mahadasha}) \times 19(\text{Jupiter's Mahadasha})}{108(\text{total wheel of life})}$$

$$= \frac{15 \times 19}{108} = \frac{285}{108} \text{ years}$$

$$= \frac{285}{108} \times 12 = 31 \text{ months} + 20 \text{ days, i.e. } 2 \text{ years} + 7 \text{ months} + 20 \text{ days.}$$

Example no. 2:- Antardasha of Moon in Saturn:–

$$\frac{15 \times 10 \times 12}{108} = \frac{50}{3} \text{ months} = 16 \text{ months} + 20 \text{ days, i.e. } 1 \text{ year} + 4 \text{ months} + 20 \text{ days.}$$

{For details please refer to Appendix – 2 (Ashtottari System)}.

Appendix – 1 (Vimshottri System)

Ready reckoner showing the Mahadasha period and the Antardasha periods (sub periods) of a planet:

1. Sun (6 Years)				2. Moon (10 years)				3. Mars (7 years)			
	year	month	day		year	month	day		year	month	day
Sun	0	3	18	Moon	0	10	0	Mars	0	4	27
Moon	0	6	0	Mars	0	7	0	Rahu	1	0	18
Mars	0	4	6	Rahu	1	6	0	Jupiter	0	11	6
Rahu	0	10	24	Jupiter	1	4	0	Saturn	1	1	9
Jupiter	0	9	18	Saturn	1	7	0	Mercury	0	11	27
Saturn	0	11	12	Mercury	1	5	0	Ketu	0	4	27
Mercury	0	10	6	Ketu	0	7	0	Venus	1	2	0
Ketu	0	4	6	Venus	1	8	0	Sun	0	4	6
Venus	1	0	0	Sun	0	6	0	Moon	0	7	0

4. Rahu (18 Years)	year	month	day	5. Jupiter (16 years)	year	month	day	6. Saturn (19 years)	year	month	day
Rahu	2	8	12	Jupiter	2	1	18	Saturn	3	0	3
Jupiter	2	4	24	Saturn	2	6	12	Mercury	2	8	9
Saturn	2	10	6	Mercury	2	3	6	Ketu	1	1	9
Mercury	2	6	18	Ketu	0	11	6	Venus	3	2	0
Ketu	1	0	18	Venus	2	8	0	Sun	0	11	12
Venus	3	0	0	Sun	0	9	18	Moon	1	7	0
Sun	0	10	24	Moon	1	4	0	Mars	1	1	9
Moon	1	6	0	Mars	0	11	6	Rahu	2	10	6
Mars	1	0	18	Rahu	2	4	24	Jupiter	2	6	12

7. Mercury (17 Years)	year	month	day	8. Ketu (7 years)	year	month	day	9. Venus (20 years)	year	month	day
Mercury	2	4	27	Ketu	0	4	27	Venus	3	4	0
Ketu	0	11	27	Venus	1	2	0	Sun	1	0	0
Venus	2	10	0	Sun	0	4	6	Moon	1	8	0
Sun	0	10	6	Moon	0	7	0	Mars	1	2	0
Moon	1	5	0	Mars	0	4	27	Rahu	3	0	0
Mars	0	11	27	Rahu	1	0	18	Jupiter	2	8	0
Rahu	2	6	18	Jupiter	0	11	6	Saturn	3	2	0
Jupiter	2	3	6	Saturn	1	1	9	Mercury	2	10	0
Saturn	2	8	9	Mercury	0	11	27	Ketu	1	2	0

Appendix – 2 (Ashtottari System)

Sub-periods in Dasha of Sun (6 Years)

Planet	Sun	Moon	Mars	Mercury	Saturn	Jupiter	Rahu	Venus
Year	0	0	0	0	0	1	0	1
Month	4	10	5	11	6	0	8	2
Day	0	0	10	10	20	20	0	0

Sub-periods in Dasha of Moon (15 Years)

Planet	Moon	Mars	Mercury	Saturn	Jupiter	Rahu	Venus	Sun
Year	2	1	2	1	2	1	2	0
Month	1	1	4	4	7	8	11	10
Day	0	10	10	20	20	0	0	0

Sub-periods in Dasha of Mars (8 Years)

Planet	Mars	Mercury	Saturn	Jupiter	Rahu	Venus	Sun	Moon
Year	0	1	0	1	0	1	0	1
Month	7	3	8	4	10	6	5	1
Day	3	3	26	26	20	10	10	10
Ghati	20	20	40	40	0	0	0	0

Sub-periods in Dasha of Mercury (17 Years)

Planet	Mercury	Saturn	Jupiter	Rahu	Venus	Sun	Moon	Mars
Year	2	1	2	1	3	0	2	1
Month	8	6	11	10	3	11	4	3
Day	3	26	26	20	20	10	10	3
Ghati	20	40	40	0	0	0	-	20

Sub-periods in Dasha of Saturn (10 Years)

Planet	Saturn	Jupiter	Rahu	Venus	Sun	Moon	Mars	Mercury
Year	0	1	1	1	0	1	0	1
Month	11	9	1	11	6	4	8	6
Day	3	3	10	10	20	20	26	26
Ghati	20	20	0	0	0	0	40	40

Sub-periods in Dasha of Jupiter (19 Years)

Planet	Jupiter	Rahu	Venus	Sun	Moon	Mars	Mercury	Saturn
Year	3	2	3	1	2	1	2	1
Month	4	1	8	0	7	4	11	9
Day	3	10	10	20	20	26	26	3
Ghati	20	0	0	0	0	40	40	20

Sub-periods in Dasha of Rahu (12 Years)

Planet	Rahu	Venus	Sun	Moon	Mars	Mercury	Saturn	Jupiter
Year	1	2	0	1	0	1	1	2
Month	4	4	8	8	10	10	1	1
Day	0	0	0	0	20	20	10	10
Ghati	0	0	0	0	0	0	0	0

Sub-periods in Dasha of Venus (21 Years)

Planet	Venus	Sun	Moon	Mars	Mercury	Saturn	Jupiter	Rahu
Year	4	1	2	1	3	1	3	2
Month	1	2	11	6	3	11	8	4
Day	0	0	0	20	20	10	10	0
Ghati	0	0	0	0	0	0	0	0

Yogini Dasha (36 years cycle of Planets):

This system is equally important in making comprehensive judgement of a Birth chart. It extends to 36 years and repeats itself after every 36 years. If the first 36 years have given adverse effects, the next 36 years will not be malefic as all such malefic planets lose their sting. Like Vimoshottari and Ashtottari systems of Mahadasha, this system is also based on constellation or Nakshatra occupied by Moon at the time of birth. Formula for calculating this system of Mahadasha is the same as in the other systems enumerated in previous pages. In the table following are the names of Yogini Dashas and the planets Lords presiding over those Dashas.

Yogini Dasha Table for Birth Nakshatras

Name	Planet	Years	Nakshatras
Mangala	Moon	1	Ardra, Chitra, Shravana
Pingala	Sun	2	P.Vasu, Swati, Dhanishta
Dhanya	Jupiter	3	Pushya, Vishakha, Shatbhisha
Bhramari	Mars	4	Ashlesha, Anu, P.Bh., Ashwani
Bhadra	Mercury	5	Magha, Jyeshta, U.Bh., Bharni
Ulka	Saturn	6	P.Phal., Mool, Revati, Kritika
Sidha	Venus	7	U.Phal, P. Shada, Rohini
Sankata	Rahu / Ketu	8	Hastha, U. Shada, Mrigshira

Calculation of Yogini Antardasha:

(Lord of Main Dasha × Sub-period of Lord) / 36

Example: To calculate the sub-period of Saturn (Ulka) in Jupiter (Dhanya):

(3×6)/36 = ½ years, i.e. 6 months.

Or

To calculate the sub-period of Venus (Sidha) in Mercury (Bhadra):

(5×7)/36 = 35/36 years = (35×12 months)/36

= 35/3 months = 11 months and 20 days.

Effect of Mahadasha and Antardasha:

1. It must be noted that during the main period or Dasha of an exalted / benefic planet, the results are exalted and good; but the Antardasha also plays a major role in conferring good or bad effect. Though Mahadasha is of an exalted planet, yet if the sub-period is of an enemy planet, the good effect is marred and vitiated.

Example: It is Moon's Dasha of ten years and Moon is exalted; if it passes through the Antardasha of Saturn, the results are malefic, as Saturn destroys Moon. The man suffers for one year and seven months. Even the Pratyantar dasha, i.e. sub-sub-period also plays a significant role. For 3 months and 3 days (Saturn's Pratyantar in Moon), the results are the worst; but later on there may be some respite, but overall period of 1 year and 7 months is not good. So is the case with all other planets, their Dashas and Antardashas and Pratyantar dashas.

2. Conclusions to be drawn:

(a) In the Mahadasha of an exalted / benefic planet, overall results are exalted / good; provided the Antardasha is also of a friendly planet or its own. When a powerful enemy planet's Antardasha intervenes, the good effect is somewhat nullified.

(b) In the Mahadasha of a malefic planet and malefic Antardasha, one loses a lot by way of wealth, health and reputation.

(c) In the Mahadasha of a malefic planet, but Antardasha of a benefic planet, results will be partially bad and partially all right, as a rogue never abandons the path of evil.

(d) During the Antardasha of an enemy planet, in the debilitated planet, the results are disastrous in every respect.

Note: The effect of Pratyantar dasha, i.e. sub-sub-period, though extending to just a few months or days, may not be lost sight of. It does have some effect – good or bad.

Sade-sati (7 ½ years of most malefic influence of Saturn):

"Nothing is permanent in this wicked world, not even our troubles."

– Charlie Chaplin.

In Hindu Astrology, Saturn plays a very vital role in man's life – good or bad. When an astrologer talks of "Sade-sati", it sends shivers down the spine of the client. He at once appeals to the astrologer to devise some means to extricate him from the clutches of Saturn's most obnoxious attacks. Let me apprise you of the malefic as well as benefic characteristics of Saturn. It is a double edged weapon – both protector as well as destroyer. It is the most malefic in Aries and most exalted in Libra. Capricorn and Aquarius are its own Raashis or signs, but in enemy's sign or House it wreaks havoc and spreads destruction all around. It destroys the enemy Raashis. Its friends are Venus and Mercury; but its sworn enemies are Sun, Moon and Mars, i.e. Aries, Cancer, Leo, and Scorpio are its foes. Jupiter – of course, is of equal strength. Its aspects are 3rd, 7th and 10th from the House which it occupies. It is the Lord of Capricorn and Aquarius which extend from 270 to 300 degrees and 300 to 330 degrees respectively.

It may be noted that Saturn in Jupiter's sign, i.e. Sagittarius and Pisces, is benefic; whereas Jupiter in Saturn's sign, i.e. Capricorn is debilitated and weak.

Everyone has to pass through this fire; some are burnt and scalded and some come out unscathed like metal turning into gold. For some with malefic Saturn it is all poison and venom; but for those with exalted Saturn it is all fine. It may be noted that **Sun remains in one sign for 1 month; Moon for 2¼ days; Mars for 1½ months; Jupiter for 13 months; Venus and Mercury for 1 month; Rahu and Ketu (retrograde) for 18 months moving backwards; but Saturn's sojourn in one sign is for 30 months.**

People with malefic Saturn are cheats, indolent, lazy, thief, liar, jealous, subtle like snake, notorious, callous and cruel, full of anger and venom, stubborn, secretive, but self-respecting, may break but will never bend before enemies; hit back with vigour when insulted; terror for their foes. Even in day-to-day dealings, such persons are peevish and quarrelsome.

Here is the chart showing period of "Sade-sati" and "Dhayas" (2½ years of Saturn's stay in a particular Raashi):

S.No.	Sign (Raashi)	Sign (Raashi)		
		First 2 ½ years	Second 2 ½ years	Third 2 ½ Years
1.	Aries (1)	Pisces (12)	Aries (1)	Taurus (2)
2	Taurus (2)	Aries (1)	Taurus (2)	Gemini (3)
3	Gemini (3)	Taurus (2)	Gemini (3)	Cancer (4)
4	Cancer (4)	Gemini (3)	Cancer (4)	Leo (5)
5	Leo (5)	Cancer (4)	Leo (5)	Virgo (6)
6	Virgo (6)	Leo (5)	Virgo (6)	Libra (7)
7	Libra (7)	Virgo (6)	Libra (7)	Scorpio (8)
8	Scorpio (8)	Libra (7)	Scorpio (8)	Sagittarius (9)
9	Sagittarius (9)	Scorpio (8)	Sagittarius (9)	Capricorn (10)
10	Capricorn (10)	Sagittarius (9)	Capricorn (10)	Aquarius (11)
11	Aquarius (11)	Capricorn (10)	Aquarius (11)	Pisces (12)
12	Pisces (12)	Aquarius (11)	Pisces (12)	Aries (1)

Number in brackets indicates Raashi's number. I have mentioned them to facilitate memorising them. Aries is no.1 Raashi; Taurus is no.2; so on and so forth.

Example: Suppose Saturn is passing through Cancer (Raashi no.4); it will affect three Raashis simultaneously, i.e. Gemini (3), Cancer (4) and Leo (5), i.e. it will affect not only the Raashi of its sojourn but also one behind and one ahead. This is how Saturn strikes. Besides the above three Raashis, it also hurts the 6th and 9th Raashi from self. These are called Dhayas, i.e. 2½ years of Saturn's poisonous arrows.

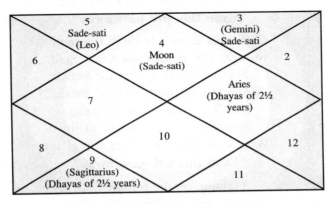

Thus we have noted that Saturn affects five signs simultaneously. If Saturn stays in a friendly sign, it may hiss and spread terror in the mind, i.e. man may be tense and depressed but it never hurts a friend in the end. Rogues have their own code of conduct, i.e. they never betray their friends. If Saturn passes through an enemy Raashi, it destroys it lock, stock and barrel.

Remedy lies in facing this period with stoic courage, for after this dark period, again there will be sunshine and glory. My advice is "Never lose heart, face it boldly and cheerfully, for life is a web of grief and happiness. Have you ever known a man, howsoever eminent, who has not suffered in life?"

Apart from meditation, do good to all; imbibe noble thoughts; donate milk (Moon's articles) and almonds, iron plate or iron tongs or coconut (Saturn's articles) to the needy and the poor.

This will boost your morale and will strengthen your resolve to steer clear of this trap of malefic Saturn.

Let me also refer to the following words of advice:

> "Once in Persia reigned a king,
>   Who upon a signet ring
> Graved a maxim true and wise,
> Which, if held before his eyes,
> Gave him counsel at a glance,
> Fit for every change and chance,
> Solemn words and these are they,
> **"Even this will pass away".**
>
> Trains of camels through the sand
> Brought him gems from Samarcand;
>   Fleets of galleys over the seas
>   Brought him pearls to rival these,
> But he counted not his gain,
> Treasures of the mine or main;
> "What is wealth?" the king would say,
> **"Even this will pass away".**
>
> Fighting on the furious field,
> Once a javelin pierced his shield,
> Soldiers, with a loud lament,
> Bore him bleeding to his tent.
> Groaning from his tortured side,
> "Pain is hard to bear", he cried,
> But with patience, day by day,
> **"Even this will pass away".**
>
> Towering in a public square
>   Twenty cubits in the air,
> Rose his statue, carved in stone.
> Then the king disguised, unknown,
> Stood before his sculptured name,
> Musing meekly: "What is fame?"
>   Fame is but a slow decay!
> **"Even this will pass away".**

Struck with palsy, sore and old,
Waiting at the Gates of Gold,
Said he with dying breath
"Life is done, but what is Death?"
Then, in answer to the king
Fell a sunbeam on his ring;
Showing by a heavenly ray,
"Even this will pass away".

— **Theodore Tilton**

❖◆❖

CHAPTER 27

Varsh Phal

Annual Results (Varsh Phal):

There are many methods to work out the Annual results in the life of an individual; whether you adopt the formula enunciated by the ancient astrologers or in the Lal Kitab of Astrology, results are the same.

Here is the formula followed by astrologers for ascertaining the Annual chart of an individual:

(1) Date of Birth: 23-11-1969

(2) Day and Time of Birth: Sunday at 15:40 hrs.

Let us find out the Annual chart for the year 2005:

(1) Deduct the birth year from 2005:   2005-1969 = 36 years

(2) Find out days, months and minutes from the appended chart of "Annual Sarni" against 36 years:

It is 3 days 5 hours and 30 minutes

(3) Add the above to native's day and time of birth:

	Days	Hours	Minutes
	3	05	30
	1	15	40
Total	**4**	**21**	**10**

(Taking 1 as Sunday, 2 as Monday, 3 as Tuesday, 4 as Wednesday, 5 as Thursday, 6 as Friday, 7 or 0 as Saturday)

It comes to Wednesday at 21 hours and 10 minutes.

Now find out from "Lagna Sarni" (available in all Panchangs or ephemerides). It is calculated Cancer (4) as Lagna or Ascendant. Now prepare the Annual chart for 23rd Nov., 2005 at 21 hrs 10 minutes. As regards "Muntha", add the previous years, i.e. 35 years to Lagna Raashi, i.e. Aries (1) = 36; divide the total by 12. The remainder is zero, i.e. 12; write "Muntha" against the remainder, i.e. 12.

Birth Chart:

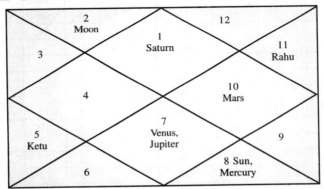

Annual Chart:

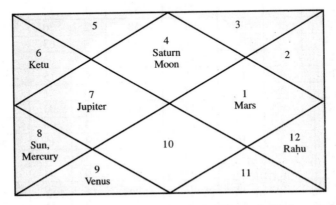

Effect of Muntha in No. 1, 2, 3, 5, 9, 10, and 11 is good.

Effect of Muntha in No. 4, 6, 7, 8 and 12 is bad.

Chart of Annual Sarni:

Previous Year	Days	Hours	Minutes	Previous Year	Day	Hours	Minutes
1	1	06	09	36	3	05	30
2	2	12	18	37	4	11	39
3	3	18	27	38	5	17	48
4	5	00	37	39	6	23	57
5	6	06	46	40	1	06	07
6	0	12	55	41	2	12	16
7	1	19	04	42	3	18	25
8	3	01	13	43	5	00	34
9	4	07	23	44	6	06	43
10	5	13	32	45	0	12	42
11	6	19	41	46	1	19	02
12	1	01	50	47	3	01	11
13	2	07	59	48	4	07	20
14	3	14	08	49	5	13	29
15	4	20	17	50	6	19	38
16	6	02	27	51	1	01	47
17	0	08	36	52	2	07	57
18	1	14	45	53	3	14	06
19	2	20	54	54	4	20	15
20	4	03	03	55	6	02	24
21	5	09	12	56	0	08	33
22	6	15	22	57	1	14	42
23	0	21	31	58	2	20	51
24	2	03	40	59	4	03	01
25	3	09	49	60	5	09	10
26	4	15	58	61	6	15	19
27	5	22	07	62	0	21	28
28	0	04	17	63	2	03	37
29	1	10	26	64	3	06	43
30	2	16	35	65	4	15	56
31	3	22	44	66	5	22	05
32	5	04	53	67	0	04	14
33	6	11	02	68	1	10	23
34	0	17	32	69	2	16	32
35	1	23	21	70	3	22	41

Previous Year	Days	Hours	Minutes	Previous Year	Day	Hours	Minutes
71	5	04	51	86	3	01	08
72	6	11	00	87	4	07	17
73	0	17	09	88	5	13	26
74	1	23	18	89	6	19	36
75	3	05	27	90	1	01	45
76	4	11	36	91	2	07	54
77	5	17	46	92	3	14	03
78	6	23	55	93	4	20	12
79	1	06	04	94	6	02	21
80	2	12	13	95	0	08	30
81	3	18	22	96	1	14	40
82	5	00	34	97	2	20	49
83	6	06	41	98	4	20	58
84	0	12	50	99	5	09	07
85	1	18	59	100	6	15	16

I have given this for academic discussion; otherwise all are available in computerised horoscopes, Annual charts and Panchangs. I have thoroughly studied Lal Kitab in Urdu and translated it into English and have come to the conclusion that Annual charts given in the next few pages, based on Lal Kitab are also very effective and correct.

Here is the catalogue of Annual charts from Lal Kitab:

Houses

AGE	1	2	3	4	5	6	7	8	9	10	11	12
1	1	9	10	3	5	2	11	7	6	12	4	8
2	4	1	12	9	3	7	5	6	2	8	10	11
3	9	4	1	2	8	3	10	5	7	11	12	6
4	3	8	4	1	10	9	6	11	5	7	2	12
5	11	3	8	4	1	5	9	2	12	6	7	10
6	5	12	3	8	4	11	2	9	1	10	6	7
7	7	6	9	5	12	4	1	10	11	2	8	3
8	2	7	6	12	9	10	3	1	8	5	11	4
9	12	2	7	6	11	1	8	4	10	3	5	9
10	10	11	2	7	6	12	4	8	3	1	9	5
11	8	5	11	10	7	6	12	3	9	4	1	2

Contd....

AGE	1	2	3	4	5	6	7	8	9	10	11	12
12	6	10	5	11	2	8	7	12	4	9	3	1
13	1	5	10	8	11	6	7	2	12	3	9	4
14	4	1	3	2	5	7	8	11	6	12	10	9
15	9	4	1	6	8	5	2	7	11	10	12	3
16	3	9	4	1	12	8	6	5	2	7	11	10
17	11	3	9	4	1	10	5	6	7	8	2	12
18	5	11	6	9	4	1	12	8	10	2	3	7
19	7	10	11	3	9	4	1	12	8	5	6	2
20	2	7	5	12	3	9	10	1	4	6	8	11
21	12	2	8	5	10	3	9	4	1	11	7	6
22	10	12	2	7	6	11	3	9	5	1	4	8
23	8	6	12	10	7	2	11	3	9	4	1	5
24	6	8	7	11	2	12	4	10	3	9	5	1
25	1	6	10	3	2	8	7	4	11	5	12	9
26	4	1	3	8	6	7	2	11	12	9	5	10
27	9	4	1	5	10	11	12	7	6	8	2	3
28	3	9	4	1	11	5	6	8	7	2	10	12
29	11	3	9	4	1	6	8	2	10	12	7	5
30	5	11	8	9	4	1	3	12	2	10	6	7
31	7	5	11	12	9	4	1	10	8	6	3	2
32	2	7	5	11	3	12	10	6	4	1	9	8
33	12	2	6	10	8	3	9	1	5	7	4	11
34	10	12	2	7	5	9	11	3	1	4	8	6
35	8	10	12	6	7	2	4	5	9	3	11	1
36	6	8	7	2	12	10	5	9	3	11	1	4
37	1	3	10	6	9	12	7	5	11	2	4	8
38	4	1	3	8	6	5	2	7	12	10	11	9
39	9	4	1	12	8	2	10	11	6	3	5	7
40	3	9	4	1	11	8	6	12	2	5	7	10
41	11	7	9	4	1	6	8	2	10	12	3	5
42	5	11	8	9	12	1	3	4	7	6	10	2
43	7	5	11	2	3	4	1	10	8	9	12	6
44	2	10	5	3	4	9	12	8	1	7	6	11
45	12	2	6	5	10	7	9	1	3	11	8	4
46	10	12	2	7	5	3	11	6	4	8	9	1
47	8	6	12	10	7	11	4	9	5	1	2	3
48	6	8	7	11	2	10	5	3	9	4	1	12
49	1	7	10	6	12	2	8	4	11	9	3	5
50	4	1	8	3	6	12	5	11	2	7	10	9

Contd....

AGE	1	2	3	4	5	6	7	8	9	10	11	12
51	9	4	1	2	8	3	12	6	7	10	5	11
52	3	9	4	1	11	7	2	12	5	8	6	10
53	11	10	7	4	1	6	3	9	12	5	8	2
54	5	11	3	9	4	1	6	2	10	12	7	8
55	7	5	11	8	3	9	1	10	6	4	2	12
56	2	3	5	11	9	4	10	1	8	6	12	7
57	12	2	6	5	10	8	9	7	4	11	1	3
58	10	12	2	7	5	11	4	8	3	1	9	6
59	8	6	12	10	7	5	11	3	9	2	4	1
60	6	8	9	12	2	10	7	5	1	3	11	4
61	1	11	10	6	12	2	4	7	8	9	5	3
62	4	1	6	8	3	12	2	10	9	5	7	11
63	9	4	1	2	8	6	12	11	7	3	10	5
64	3	9	4	1	6	8	7	12	5	2	11	10
65	11	2	9	4	1	5	8	3	10	12	6	7
66	5	10	3	9	2	1	6	8	11	7	12	4
67	7	5	11	3	10	4	1	9	12	6	8	2
68	2	3	5	11	9	7	10	1	6	8	4	12
69	12	8	7	5	11	3	9	4	1	10	2	6
70	10	12	2	7	5	11	3	6	4	1	9	8
71	8	6	12	10	7	9	11	5	2	4	3	1
72	6	7	8	12	4	10	5	2	3	11	1	9
73	1	4	10	6	12	11	7	8	2	5	9	3
74	4	2	3	8	6	12	1	11	7	10	5	9
75	9	10	1	3	8	6	2	7	5	4	12	11
76	3	9	6	1	2	8	5	12	11	7	10	4
77	11	3	9	4	1	2	8	10	12	6	7	5
78	5	11	4	9	7	1	6	2	10	12	3	8
79	7	5	11	2	9	4	12	6	3	1	8	10
80	2	8	5	11	4	7	10	3	1	9	6	12
81	12	1	7	5	11	10	9	4	8	3	2	6
82	10	12	2	7	5	3	4	9	6	8	11	1
83	8	6	12	10	3	5	11	1	9	2	4	7
84	6	7	8	12	10	9	3	5	4	11	1	2
85	1	3	10	6	12	2	8	6	5	4	9	7
86	4	1	8	3	6	12	11	2	7	9	10	5
87	9	4	1	7	3	8	12	5	2	6	11	10
88	3	9	4	1	8	10	2	7	12	5	6	11
89	11	10	9	4	1	6	7	12	3	8	5	2

Contd....

AGE	1	2	3	4	5	6	7	8	9	10	11	12
90	5	11	6	9	4	1	3	8	10	2	7	12
91	7	5	11	2	10	4	6	9	8	3	12	1
92	2	7	5	11	9	3	10	4	1	12	8	6
93	12	8	7	5	2	11	9	1	6	10	3	4
94	10	12	2	8	11	5	4	6	9	7	1	3
95	8	6	12	10	5	7	1	3	4	11	2	9
96	6	2	3	12	7	9	5	10	11	1	4	8
97	1	9	10	6	12	2	7	5	3	4	8	11
98	4	1	6	8	10	12	11	2	9	7	3	5
99	9	4	1	2	6	8	12	11	5	3	10	7
100	3	10	8	1	5	7	6	12	2	9	11	4
101	11	3	9	4	1	6	8	10	7	5	12	2
102	5	11	3	9	4	1	2	6	8	12	7	10
103	7	5	11	3	9	4	1	8	12	10	2	6
104	2	7	5	11	3	9	10	1	6	8	4	12
105	12	2	4	5	11	3	9	4	10	6	1	8
106	10	12	2	7	8	5	3	9	4	11	6	1
107	8	6	12	10	7	11	4	3	1	2	5	9
108	6	8	7	12	2	10	5	4	11	1	9	3
109	1	9	10	6	12	2	7	11	5	3	4	8
110	4	1	6	8	10	12	3	5	7	2	11	9
111	9	4	1	2	5	8	12	10	6	7	3	11
112	3	10	8	9	11	7	4	1	2	12	6	5
113	11	3	9	4	1	6	2	7	10	5	8	12
114	5	11	3	1	4	10	6	8	12	9	7	2

It is very easy to understand the results as per the Annual chart.

Annual Chart:

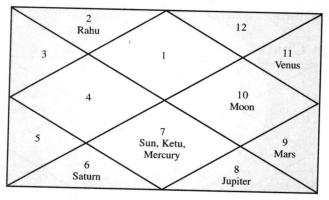

Predictions:

1. Exalted Rahu in House no.2 confers exalted status.
2. Exalted Saturn will confer best results.
3. Sun in House no.7 may create problems in career in the 7th month.
4. Mars in House no.9 will confer good results.
5. Moon though malefic is aspected by Saturn – in its sign.
6. Venus will confer best results.

Note: Don't forget to see aspects.

Marriage Yoga according to Annual results from Lal Kitab:

When Saturn favourably aspects Venus; or Venus and Mercury favourably aspect each other or when Saturn occupies House no.1 or 7 in the Annual chart, Marriage Yoga may be predicted.

OR

When Venus or Mercury occupies House no.1, Marriage Yoga can be predicted.

OR

Venus and Mercury occupy the same House in which they are placed in the Birth chart, Marriage Yoga may be predicted.

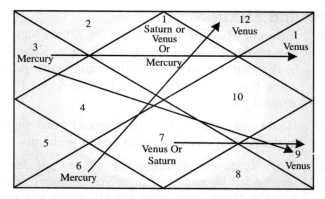

In all the above cases, Marriage Yoga is formed.

Note: If Sun occupies House no. 6 and Saturn House no.12 in the Annual chart **OR** Sun occupies House no.1 and Saturn House no.8 in the Annual chart, Spouse may suffer; it may lead to separation or even death.

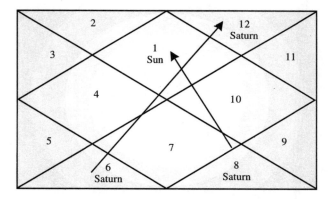

Illness and Sickness:

(a) If Sun or Moon is associated with Venus, Mercury or any of the wicked planets, i.e. Saturn, Rahu / Ketu in the Birth chart, they will create health problems when they occupy House no.1, 6, 7, 8 and 10 in the Annual chart.

(b) House no.3 or House no.8, if occupied by malefic planets in the Annual chart, signifies health problems.

(c) There is danger to life every 8th year, if Jupiter is surrounded by enemy planets viz; Mercury, Venus or Rahu in House no.9 or sign no.9; also when Moon – Rahu are in no.7 or 8 and also when Mercury is in no.9 (House or Sign) with Jupiter, but Jupiter saves the man.

―――――❖◆❖―――――

Diseases Caused by Malefic Planets

Malefic Planet	Diseases
Malefic Jupiter	Asthma
Malefic Sun	Loss of sensation in the limbs; irregular heart beat
Malefic Moon	Epilepsy; fits; insanity; eye problem; heart problem
Malefic Mars	Stomach ache; ulcer; liver trouble; boils; uterus problem in ladies
Malefic Venus	Skin disease; boils etc.
Malefic Mercury	Disease of brain; insensitive to smell; disease of teeth and veins
Malefic Rahu	Disease of brain, accidents, fever, bad for career
Malefic Ketu	Arthritis, urinary trouble, ear problems; hernia
Malefic Saturn	Disease of eye; cough
Malefic Jupiter – Rahu/Ketu	Asthma (remedy for Rahu)
Malefic Jupiter - Mars	Jaundice (remedy for malefic Jupiter)
Malefic Mars - Ketu	Trembling of hands, feet and head. (Remedy for malefic Mars)

These remedies for pacifying the malefic planets may be adopted for 43 days or on the days earmarked for these planets viz. Sunday,

Monday, Wednesday, Thursday, Friday and Saturday for Sun and Ketu, Moon, Mercury, Jupiter (Rahu on Thursday A.M.), Venus and Saturn respectively.

Articles to be donated to placate Planets:

Malefic Planet	Articles
Malefic Jupiter	Topaz; gold, chana daal; turmeric; saffron; yellow articles; Vishnu Worship
Malefic Sun	Ruby; copper; wheat; jaggery; Vishnu Puran.
Malefic Moon	Rice; silver, milky white pearl, white flower; white cloth; Shiva Worship.
Malefic Mars	Coral; masur daal; sugar; red cloth; red flower; Gayatri Paath.
Malefic Venus	Ghee; curd; diamond; fragrant grey white articles; selfless service of people.
Malefic Mercury	Emerald; moong; green cloth; Durga Paath
Malefic Saturn	Sapphire; iron articles viz. iron tongs, iron plate etc.; urad (black lentils); leather goods; oil; shoes; black cloth; coal; timber; respect for elders.
Malefic Jupiter – Rahu/Ketu	Remedy for Rahu
Malefic Jupiter - Mars	Remedy for malefic Jupiter
Malefic Mars - Ketu	Remedy for malefic Mars

Stars, Signs (Raashis) for diseases and remedies:

In the beginning, I have quoted Shakespeare that "Stars do govern our condition". It obviously means that what we are is the direct consequence of the movement of the planets. Now even the eminent physicians are convinced of the significance of planets not only in ascertaining our diseases, but the diet that may help restore health. Naturally the Signs (Raashis) of the Zodiac should be studied carefully and dietary supplement be recommended accordingly. Astrological medicines should become an integral part of our medical practices and system. Astrologers consider the various parts of the body as being ruled by certain signs of the Zodiac. Naturally, many diseases are associated with these signs governing a specific disease and part of body. Astrologers therefore divide the body according to the ruling signs. Following are the ailments associated with the particular signs and the recommended diets, besides the remedies suggested in previous pages. These may be followed in right perspective.

1. **Aries:** Aries is the lord of head and face. Arians often suffer from severe headache. This sign also controls adrenaline. It may cause physical problems; nervousness, tension of the mind and bad digestion. Such a person should take lots of vegetables and fruits rich in potassium, phosphate, viz. tomatoes, brown rice, beans, bananas, etc. but these should be taken in consultation with a specialist.

2. **Taurus:** This sign is the presiding lord of throat, vocal chords and neck, hence such persons are prone to bad colds and sinusitis. Astro-physicians recommend a diet rich in minerals. They also advise the patients to take a lot of water to keep the kidneys perfectly in order. Fish, cauliflower, spinach, onions, raw nuts, etc. are recommended as these are rich in minerals and iodine.

3. **Gemini:** It is the presiding lord of lungs, nerves, arms and shoulders. Such persons are prone to accidents which may break the collar bone. Doctors recommend food rich in potassium, chloride and calcium. Such a diet helps restore patient's health in matters of respiratory problems such as asthma, bronchitis, etc. Obviously, such patients are advised to take carrots, oranges, raisins, milk and cheese in plenty.

4. **Cancer:** It is the presiding sign for breast, eyes, heart, stomach and the alimentary canal. It may cause bleeding of gums, varicose veins, eyes and heart problem.

They usually suffer from indigestion and ulcers. They are generally delicate and of weak health. They are advised to take food rich in calcium, such as eggs, curd, beetroot, milk, cabbage, fish and crab.

5. **Leo:** This is the presiding Raashi for back, heart and spinal chord. Such persons are vulnerable to heart attacks. In order to control the above ailments, one should take diet rich in magnesium, phosphate and iron, viz. almonds, wheat, rice, eggs, beetroot, dates, raisins and spinach.

6. **Virgo:** This sign of the Zodiac rules over the nervous system and intestines. They are worried over trifles and hence suffer from indigestion and restlessness. Such a person may suffer from hair loss, dandruff, acne, itching, constipation, etc. Food rich in potassium, sulphate, such as leafy vegetables, lemons, almonds, curd, rice, papaya, egg, etc. are recommended.

7. **Libra:** This Raashi presides over the kidneys and hips. Although they are well balanced in their thoughts and way of life, yet are prone to kidney problem. Let us advise such persons to take food rich in sodium, phosphate, viz. apple, peas, carrots, corn, radish, tomatoes, wheat, green vegetables, salad and fresh fruit.

8. **Scorpio:** This sign is the presiding lord of sexual organs. They are over sexed and do not believe in doing things by halves, i.e. they cross the limits. Suppression of sexual desire may lead to frustration and cruel behaviour.

9. **Sagittarius:** This sign is the presiding Raashi of liver, hips and thighs. They become fat if they do not exercise regularly. Women develop flab at hips and thighs. In order to control falling of hair, skin problem, or bleeding of gums, one should take food rich in silica, high proteins, i.e. fruits, vegetables, salad, apple, potatoes and fish.

10. **Capricorn:** This is the ruling sign of bones, knees, joints and teeth. To prevent rickets, spinal, dental,

Example:

Date of Birth: April 05, 1959

Birth Chart

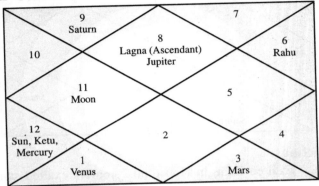

Take Lagna as the First House, prepare the following chart:

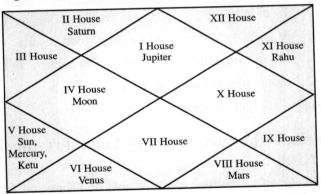

Now prepare the Annual chart for the year April 2005 – April 2006, i.e. <u>47th year</u>.

studied carefully and dietary supplement be recommended accordingly. Astrological medicines should become an integral part of our medical practices and system. Astrologers consider the various parts of the body as being ruled by certain signs of the Zodiac. Naturally, many diseases are associated with these signs governing a specific disease and part of body. Astrologers therefore divide the body according to the ruling signs. Following are the ailments associated with the particular signs and the recommended diets, besides the remedies suggested in previous pages. These may be followed in right perspective.

1. **Aries:** Aries is the lord of head and face. Arians often suffer from severe headache. This sign also controls adrenaline. It may cause physical problems; nervousness, tension of the mind and bad digestion. Such a person should take lots of vegetables and fruits rich in potassium, phosphate, viz. tomatoes, brown rice, beans, bananas, etc. but these should be taken in consultation with a specialist.

2. **Taurus:** This sign is the presiding lord of throat, vocal chords and neck, hence such persons are prone to bad colds and sinusitis. Astro-physicians recommend a diet rich in minerals. They also advise the patients to take a lot of water to keep the kidneys perfectly in order. Fish, cauliflower, spinach, onions, raw nuts, etc. are recommended as these are rich in minerals and iodine.

3. **Gemini:** It is the presiding lord of lungs, nerves, arms and shoulders. Such persons are prone to accidents which may break the collar bone. Doctors recommend food rich in potassium, chloride and calcium. Such a diet helps restore patient's health in matters of respiratory problems such as asthma, bronchitis, etc. Obviously, such patients are advised to take carrots, oranges, raisins, milk and cheese in plenty.

4. **Cancer:** It is the presiding sign for breast, eyes, heart, stomach and the alimentary canal. It may cause bleeding of gums, varicose veins, eyes and heart problem.

They usually suffer from indigestion and ulcers. They are generally delicate and of weak health. They are advised to take food rich in calcium, such as eggs, curd, beetroot, milk, cabbage, fish and crab.

5. **Leo:** This is the presiding Raashi for back, heart and spinal chord. Such persons are vulnerable to heart attacks. In order to control the above ailments, one should take diet rich in magnesium, phosphate and iron, viz. almonds, wheat, rice, eggs, beetroot, dates, raisins and spinach.

6. **Virgo:** This sign of the Zodiac rules over the nervous system and intestines. They are worried over trifles and hence suffer from indigestion and restlessness. Such a person may suffer from hair loss, dandruff, acne, itching, constipation, etc. Food rich in potassium, sulphate, such as leafy vegetables, lemons, almonds, curd, rice, papaya, egg, etc. are recommended.

7. **Libra:** This Raashi presides over the kidneys and hips. Although they are well balanced in their thoughts and way of life, yet are prone to kidney problem. Let us advise such persons to take food rich in sodium, phosphate, viz. apple, peas, carrots, corn, radish, tomatoes, wheat, green vegetables, salad and fresh fruit.

8. **Scorpio:** This sign is the presiding lord of sexual organs. They are over sexed and do not believe in doing things by halves, i.e. they cross the limits. Suppression of sexual desire may lead to frustration and cruel behaviour.

9. **Sagittarius:** This sign is the presiding Raashi of liver, hips and thighs. They become fat if they do not exercise regularly. Women develop flab at hips and thighs. In order to control falling of hair, skin problem, or bleeding of gums, one should take food rich in silica, high proteins, i.e. fruits, vegetables, salad, apple, potatoes and fish.

10. **Capricorn:** This is the ruling sign of bones, knees, joints and teeth. To prevent rickets, spinal, dental,

orthopaedic ailments, arthritis, rheumatism etc., one should take almonds, oranges, lemons, potatoes, wheat, etc. – food rich in plenty of calcium and phosphate.

11. **Aquarius:** It presides over calves, ankles and circulation system. They suffer from disease of varicose veins and arteries. They should eat diet rich in sodium, chloride, i.e. sea food, spinach, almonds and fruits like oranges and lemons.

12. **Pisces:** This sign is the lord of legs, feet, toes and mucous membrane. Pisceans have weak immune system; drugs should be given after great care and thought. Such people are advised to take eggs, grapes, oranges, lemons, etc. to overcome such ailments as low blood pressure, general debility, heart problem, inflammation of joints, etc.

Note: I personally talked to an eminent Ayurvedic physician and he corroborated the above ideas. He told me that there are three types of Doshas, i.e. natural or allergic propensities. They are vata dosha, pitta dosha and kapha dosha.

(a) **Vata Dosha:** It is caused by Gemini; Virgo; Capricorn; Scorpio and Aquarius signs. They cause all types of physical problems; poor digestion, nervous restlessness; and all types of pains; respiration and circulation. It is the most important of all the three doshas.

(b) **Pitta Dosha:** This allergic ailment is caused by Aries, Leo, Sagittarius and Scorpio Raashis. Such a person is susceptible to the problems of gastric, heart burns, gas, flatulence and ulcer. It is associated with fire and heat.

(c) **Kapha Dosh:** It is caused by Taurus, Cancer, Libra, Sagittarius and Pisces signs. It causes asthma, bronchitis, persistence cough – dry and wet – such persons are voracious eaters and hence all these problems. It is the heaviest of all the doshas.

[127]

Death:

Never predict death. Man's knowledge and vision of the "Here-After" is limited. Don't scare the patient. Death is entirely in the hands of God.

Haven't we heard of the phrase "Khhuda ki Baatein Khhuda hi Jaane" (mysterious are the ways of God). They are beyond man's comprehension.

Ghalib has rightly said, "Maut ka ik din muaain hai; Neend kyon raat bhar nahin aati" (when death's day is already fixed, why to pass sleepless nights, then).

Only God knows when a person is to leave this world, for He is the Lord of creation as well as death, i.e. He is the Lord of all the worlds.

Iqbal also said: "If you ask me about the sign of faith; when death comes to him; he should have a smile on his face".

Tao Chien (365-427), the Chinese poet said: "Give yourself to the waves of the great change; neither happy nor yet afraid; And when it is time to go, then simply go, without any unnecessary fuss."

Lord Krishna says: "For that which is born, death is certain and for the dead, birth is certain. Therefore, grieve not over that which is unavoidable" (Srimad Bhagavad Gita).

Some Prominent Yogas

1. Yoga for Throne (Singhasan Yoga):

If all the planets are positioned in the 2nd or 3rd, 6th, 8th and 12th Houses; such a man occupies an eminent position, i.e. he ascends the throne. To be precise, he may become head of a state.

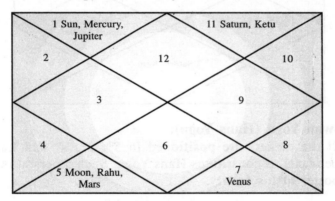

2. Yoga for Flag (Dhwaj Yoga):

If all the auspicious planets are in the Lagna and the inauspicious planets are in the 8th House in the Birth chart, it constitutes Flag Yoga. Such a person becomes an eminent leader of people, such as minister, judge or bureaucrat.

3. Ekawali Yoga (Exalted Yoga):

If all the planets are in quick succession in a Birth chart, it constitutes Ekawali Yoga. Such a person becomes very rich and head of an organisation, army or civil services.

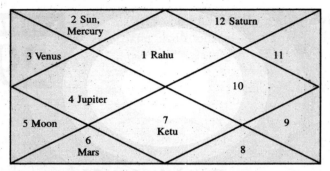

4. Chatu-Saar Yoga (Yoga for wealth):

If all the planets are in the four Kendras i.e. 1st, 4th, 7th, 10th Houses, it constitutes yoga for wealth, i.e. such a person, though born poor, becomes fabulously rich.

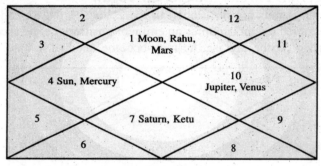

5. Swan Yoga (Hans Yoga):

If all the planets are positioned in 5th, 7th, 9th and Lagna (Ascendant), it constitutes Hans Yoga. Such a person is the supporter of his family.

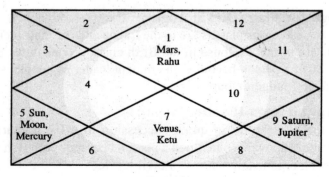

6. Swan Yoga (2) {Hans Yoga (2)}:

If all the planets in the Birth chart are in Aries (1), Libra (7), Scorpio (8) Sagittarius (9), Capricorn (10) and Aquarius (11), it forms Swan Yoga. Such a person enjoys the confidence of the powers and is the master of estates and a lot of wealth.

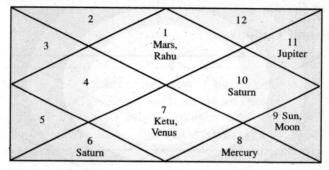

7. Karika Yoga:

If all the planets are in the 10th and 11th Houses or in the Lagna and 7th Houses, it forms Karika Yoga. Such a person, though born poor occupies an exalted status.

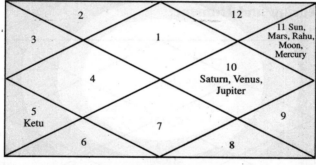

OR

Naturally, Rahu and Ketu will be at an 180° from each other.

8. Amar Yoga (Bad and Good):

If all the inauspicious <u>OR</u> auspicious planets are in the Kendras (1st, 4th, 7th, 10th Houses) – it constitutes Amar Yoga (Bad or Good).

Cruel and Callous :

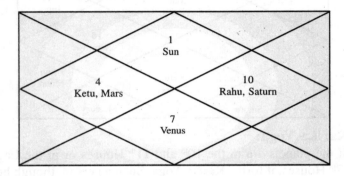

OR

God-fearing and Humane:

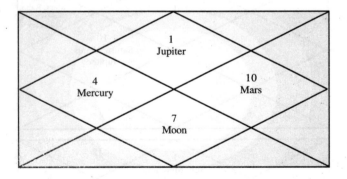

9. Chap Yoga:

If Mars is in Aries (1); Venus in Libra (7) and Jupiter in its own Raashi or sign, i.e. Leo or Sagittarius or Pisces (5, 9, and 12); such a person becomes a ruler or head of an organisation.

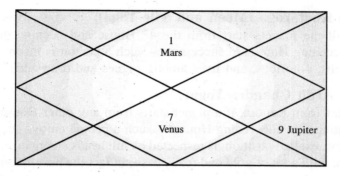

10. Dand Yoga (Exalted):

If all the planets are in Gemini (3); Cancer (4); Virgo (6); Sagittarius (9) and Pisces (12), such a person occupies the seat of justice.

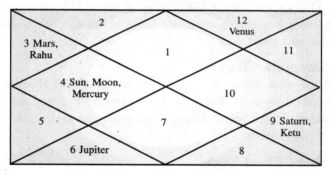

Some other Yogas:

11. Shakti Yoga:

If all the seven planets including Sun are in the 7th, 8th, 9th or 10th Houses, such a person is a fighter but lazy, indolent, grief-stricken, argumentative and always unhappy and sad.

12. Nauka Yoga (Boat Yoga):

Starting from Lagna, if all the seven planets are in all the seven Houses in succession, such a person is very popular, wealthy but greedy, clever and devoid of all pleasures.

13. Dand Yoga (Malefic):

If all the seven planets are in the 10th, 11th, 12th and 1st Houses, such a person is poor, rogue, mean and devoid of all pleasures and marital happiness. He opposes all his family members.

14. Koot Yoga (Mean and Vile Yoga):

If all the planets start from the 4th House and occupy all the succeeding Houses in succession – such a person is mean, vile, atheist, notorious, and lives among rogues and drug addicts.

15. Ardh Chandra Yoga:

Apart from Kendra, if a planet starts from any other House and continues in succeeding Houses – such a person enjoys eminent status, exalted position; is respected by all; heads an organisation; rich; with a lot of gold and ready cash; in fact the best placement of planets.

16. Chakra Yoga:

Starting from Lagna, if all the planets occupy House no.1, 3, 5, 7, 9, 11 consecutively, Chakra Yoga is formed. Such a person is handsome; patient; contented; large-hearted; compassionate; popular and good-doer.

17. Samundar Yoga:

If all the planets are in 2nd, 4th, 6th, 8th, 10th, 12th Houses, then Samundar Yoga is formed. The person is compassionate, kind-hearted; benevolent, full of contentment, good-doer and enjoys respect and esteem.

18. Short Lived Yoga:

If there is Moon in the 7th House from Lagna; with a wicked planet in 8th House and an auspicious planet and Sun in the Lagna, such a child meets an early death.

19. Illness Yoga:

If Jupiter is surrounded by wicked/enemy planets such as Rahu, Venus, Mercury – such a person falls ill, on his 8th day or month or year, i.e. 1, 8, 16, 32, 48, 56, 64, 72 years, etc.

I have explained above some of the most important yogas. There are many more but I have not intentionally referred to them, as they are beyond the scope of this book.

Gems and Precious Stones

Since ancient times, mankind has been fascinated by gems and precious stones. We hear legends and myths lauding the curative powers of the gems. We have 'Kohinoor' – the most precious diamond – adorning the crown of the queen of England. We have also heard of the worst devastating effect of the 'Hope Diamond' or the 'Diamond of Doom' – which destroyed all the families that possessed it. Thus gems can portend bad days and also usher in good days for the man who wears them. These gems are like double-edged weapons – good for some and bad for others. They should be worn judiciously and under the expert guidance of an astrologer. The aspects of various planets should also be taken into account before giving one's opinion on the gems to be worn. Further, the purity of the gem should be ascertained first before wearing it, because a faulty gem can do a lot of harm. Better to be without a gem than to wear a defective one.

S. No.	Name of Planet	Name of Gem	Attributes	Disease to be cured	When and How to wear	Time	Remarks
1.	Sun	Ruby (Manik)	Hot stone, Name & fame, position of power, vigour; warmth, symbol of love & passion	Ulcer, fever, arthritis, gout, rheumatism, etc., loss of sensation in limbs	Studded in gold in the ring finger of right hand – 3 or 6 gms. in weight	Sunday 8 AM to 10 AM	It makes life "Sunny", also helps in creating equilibrium in one's life and urge for spiritualism. It, in fact, has a great

S. No.	Name of Planet	Name of Gem	Attributes	Disease to be cured	When and How to wear	Time	Remarks
							harmonising influence upon man's life. Ordinarily it should not be worn by ladies. It is a hot gem and may make them short-- tempered & haughty and may also destroy their physical charm. Its prolonged use is also not recommended as it may cause boils, itching & insomnia. Must consult an expert astrologer before wearing it.
2.	Jupiter	Topaz (Pukhraj)	Plenty of wealth, name & fame, for a good match, cold gem, protects against all misfortunes, sadness, nervousness, etc.	Vision, asthma, ulcer, jaundice, insomnia, gastritis, stomach ailments, gout, impotency, heart problem, pain in knees, respiratory and lung problems, varicose veins.	To be studded in gold; 7 gms.; to be worn in index or ring finger of right hand.	Thursday 6 AM to 8 AM	It can be worn by ladies who find obstacles in marriage, being a cold gem, it suits them the best. It brings refreshing sleep and calms the ruffled feelings.

S. No.	Name of Planet	Name of Gem	Attributes	Disease to be cured	When and How to wear	Time	Remarks
3.	Moon	Milky White Pearl (Moti)	Cold gem; soothing effect on tantrums, depression & tensions; morale-boosting; protective shield; inspires love; happiness & fidelity; best for happy domestic & married life.	Cures insomnia, tension, sorrows, fits, insecurity, eye & heart problems, epilepsy, stomach, heart & vaginal problems, restlessness.	To be studded in silver; to be worn in ring finger after washing it with milk or sacred Ganga water.	Monday (10 AM to 11 AM) on Poorn-mashi	In fact, it has a great calming influence upon one's life and enhances one's courage & self-esteem. Most suitable gem for ladies. It increases their physical lustre & loveliness. Best for married life. The lady becomes the darling of the husband. It also enhances the sexual strength. It has soothing influence upon troubled emotions.
4.	Venus	Diamond (Heera)	Hot gem; for the most comfortable & luxurious life; for name and fame, honour, wealth & mental happiness; for sexual potency, bringer of all goodness & protective shield against all evils & bad thoughts.	Cure of diabetes, urine problem, skin disease, sexually transmitted disease, uterus problem, eczema, ring worm, etc.	To be studded in gold or platinum; ¼ or ½ gms; middle finger of right hand.	Friday (1 PM to 3 PM) or on Amavasya	Best for artists; enhances financial prospects & sexual powers; it being a hot gem. It helps inner vision, enhances psychic faculties.

S. No.	Name of Planet	Name of Gem	Attributes	Disease to be cured	When and How to wear	Time	Remarks
5.	Mars	Red Coral (Moonga)	It is red in colour, infuses courage & strength to face enemies, ensures material comforts & financial progress.	Cure of blood related ailments, cough, fever, small and chicken pox, headache. Loss of strength & virility, boils, piles, cholera, liver troubles, ulcer, disease of womb.	To be studded in silver or copper & iron, worn on first or fourth finger. Weight should be 9 or 11 or 12 gms.	Tuesday 11 AM to 1 PM	Best for enhancement of material & financial prospects, and virility and vitality. It enhances clarity of vision and resolve to resist opposition. It also purifies blood and enhances fertility in both the sexes.
6.	Mercury	Emerald (Panna)	It enhances brain power, i.e. intuition, intelligence, memory, communication skill and power of speech. It instils determination & cures the fickleness of mind.	Cures loss of memory, stammering, small pox; diseases of the brain, teeth, mouth & veins, insensitiveness to smell; dysentery, gastric ailments, fear of evil spirits.	To be studded in gold & worn in little finger of right hand.	Wednesday between 4 PM to 6 PM.	Being an effeminate gem, it is not recommended for the newly married couples. It reduces the urge for sexual intimacy, hence may lead to domestic discord. In others, it may control mercurial personality and may promote truthfulness; may give lots of wealth to the wearer.

S. No.	Name of Planet	Name of Gem	Attributes	Disease to be cured	When and How to wear	Time	Remarks
7.	Saturn	Blue Sapphire (Mani)	Right stone for health, wealth, eminent status, longevity of life, material and domestic happiness. A cold gem; security in all matters, enhances fertility in women, removes all evil effects.	Cure for fits, swoons, loss of virility, deafness, baldness, eye ailments, cough, etc.	To be studded in Panchdhatu or gold – weight should be 5 or 7 gms. Middle finger of right hand.	Saturday evening	It is the most powerful gem and hence can have adverse effects on the wearer. Please consult an expert astrologer before wearing it. First test its efficacy for a week and then wear it. It is, however, suggested that almonds, coconut or iron articles such as iron plate, etc. may be donated to the wandering sadhus or the poor. It will give all power & wealth to the wearer.
8.	Rahu	Gomedh (Hesso-nite)	For accelerated success; provides protection from calamities and enhances public relation skill. Its colour is reddish-chocolate and is a cold gem. It increases	It is cure for disease of stomach and brain fever, plague & shield against accidents, sudden loss or injury; insanity.	To be studded in silver; weight should be 6, 11 or 13 gms; should be worn in middle finger.	Thursday Evening	Please consult an expert astrologer before wearing this stone. Better donate mustard, barley or coconut for mollifying the adverse effect of Rahu. Or throw coconut, mustard on Solar eclipse in river.

S. No.	Name of Planet	Name of Gem	Attributes	Disease to be cured	When and How to wear	Time	Remarks
			appetite virility, vitality & confers health, wealth & prosperity and above all victory over enemies.			Sunday, two hours before sun-rise.	
9.	Ketu	Cat's Eye (Lehsuniya or Vaidrya)	Hot gem; cure for Ketu's evil effects, protection against accidents & enemies, confers miraculous results, bestower of wealth in speculation, betting, gambling, stock market, etc. Protective shield against punishment & police action.	Cure for diseases of limbs, sciatica, ulcer, gout, venereal diseases, urinary troubles, cancer, ear, spinal cord troubles, worries, insanity, urge for doing evil.	To be studded in gold; weight should be 3, 5 or 7 gms; to be worn in the middle finger of the right hand.		It should be worn under expert supervision of an astrologer. Ketu means 'son' and if son goes astray, this stone may help. Better donate "black & white blanket" or 3 bananas for 48 days. Also throw coconut, mustard and sesame (til) on Solar or Lunar eclipse.
10.		Feroza (Tur-quoise) Opaque or tanslucent sky blue or greenish blue precious stone	1. If there are cases of miscarriages, tie this stone around the lady's waist. God will help and there will be no miscarriage. But it should be removed at the time of labour pain or delivery. 2. A person who keeps Feroza with him is saved from fire, lightning, enemies and burns & wounds in a scuffle or a fight. (Reference – Intkhhabul-Najoom published in 1873 in Urdu-Persian)				

Overview and Charts for Quick Reading

(This chapter has been taken from Aina-e-Kismat published in Lahore in the early 20th Century)

1. Planets and jobs assigned to them:

A. Sun: is the king emperor of all planets and commands and dominates them all.

B. Moon: is the chief minister of the king.

C. Mercury: is the advisor, scholar, 'Munshi' or deed-writer.

D. Mars: is the commander-in-chief of the army.

E. Jupiter: the great teacher and the chief adviser.

F. Saturn: is the master of estates, landlord, inhabitant of deserts.

G. Venus: is a beautiful maiden, fond of music, dance; also associated with acts of sin and lust.

H. Rahu and Ketu: perform menial and dirty jobs.

2. How to find out whether a planet is exalted or debilitated:

A. Planet in its own sign (Raashi), in Lagna is always happy and lucky.

B. Planet in an exalted sign achieves exalted status and commands respect.

[141]

C. Planet in a debilitated sign is unreliable and is responsible for its own downfall.

D. A debilitated planet in enemy's house is poor, powerless, pessimistic, helpless and a slave.

E. A setting or sinking planet (Ast) is like a dead body or mortally sick.

F. A retrograde planet becoming straight-moving (Maargi); has the power to overcome all troubles and misfortunes.

G. A slow moving planet (Mandh-gati) becoming retrograde is always troublesome and unfortunate.

H. A retrograde planet moving straight and is also 'slow-moving' is a sign of prosperity and good luck.

Thus a planet in the Birth chart in an exalted or friendly or its own sign or in association with an auspicious planet or is aspected by an auspicious planet and is not a setting or sinking one, and is in a good House or in Kendra (House no. 1,4,7 and 10) and not in House no. 6,8 and 12 is very powerful and confers all prosperity, exalted status and name and fame during its 'Dasha'.

3. Retrograde and Straight-moving (Vakri and Maargi) planets:

A. Sun and Moon are always 'Maargi'.

B. Mars, Mercury, Jupiter, Venus and Saturn are 'Vakri' off and on and are 'Maargi' some times.

C. Rahu and Ketu are always 'Vakri'.

4. Rising and Sinking Planets (Uday and Ast):

A. A planet in conjunction with Sun is a sinking planet (Ast).

B. Those planets, which are in auspicious/inauspicious or ahead or behind signs become sinking planets according to the following chart.

It may be noted that the planets are called 'Rising planets (Uday)' when their distance from the Sun is more than prescribed degree, i.e. 'Ansh'.

5. Chart showing Rising or Sinking Planets according to their prescribed degrees (Ansh):

From which planet	Name of planet	Degree (Ansh)	Particulars
From Sun	Mars	17 Degrees	Sets or sinks, if just ahead or behind
From Sun	Mercury	13 Degrees	Sets or sinks, if just ahead or behind
From Sun	Jupiter	12 Degrees	Sets or sinks, if just ahead or behind
From Sun	Venus	11 Degrees	Sets or sinks, if just ahead or behind
From Sun	Saturn	14 Degrees	Sets or sinks, if just ahead or behind

6. Rising and Setting of Moon:

Moon sets in the dark fortnight (Krishna Paksha) and rises in the bright fortnight (Shukla Paksha). Rahu and Ketu are always setting nodes. Naturally Moon, Mercury and Venus are below the region occupied by the Sun. That is why they are called 'Paschimi' or 'Magrabi' or 'Western' and are down under, i.e. 'Neeche Ke' or 'Sifli'. Mars, Jupiter and Saturn are above the Sun's sky or zone and are called 'Purvi' or 'Mashraqui' or 'Eastern' and they rise before the rising of the Sun. That is why they are called exalted, i.e. 'Ulvi' or 'Oonche darje ke'. If such a planet rises at its appointed time, it confers exalted status and if by chance, one of these planets rises after the 'setting of Sun', the native suffers from poverty, sickness and misery. If a 'Neeche Ke/Sifli' planet (i.e. Moon, Mercury or Venus) rises after the setting of Sun, it confers prosperity and good fortune, and if any one of them rises just before the dawn, the native suffers from ignominy, bad name, demotion and bad luck.

It is therefore, advisable that all the above points may be taken into consideration in the Birth and Annual charts, before making any prediction.

7. Five Stages of a Planet and their Effects:

Life of a planet can be divided into five stages according to its degree (Ansh). These stages are:

- **a.** Infant (Child)
- **b.** Boy (Tifal or Ladka)
- **c.** Youth (Jawan)
- **d.** Old Age (Vridh)
- **e.** Death (Maut)

A. A planet in an odd sign, i.e. Aries (1); Gemini (3); Leo (5); Libra (7); Sagittarius (9) and Aquarius (11) passes through the above stages as explained below:

1-6 degrees	Infancy
7-12 degrees	Boyhood
13-18 degrees	Youth
19-24 degrees	Old Age
25-30 degrees	Death bed

B. As regards the five stages of planet in even signs, i.e. Taurus (2); Cancer (4); Virgo (6); Scorpio (8); Capricorn (10) and Pisces (12), the following degrees may be taken note of:

1-6 degrees	Death bed
7-12 degrees	Old Age
13-18 degrees	Youth
19-24 degrees	Boyhood
25-30 degrees	Infancy

It may be noted that every sign has a life span of 30° (total being 30 × 12 = 360°). The above facts must also be taken into consideration, while making predictions. The reader can find such a chart in every horoscope.

Note: Planet in infancy gives nominal or marginal effect. In boyhood it is 50%; in youth it is 100%; in old age it is bad; and on death bed it is the worst.

[144]

8. Chart showing the characteristics of Planets and Signs (Raashis):

This chart may be studied thoroughly, as it contains the summary of all the information which an astrologer must have at his finger tips:

Name of Sign	Aries	Taurus	Gemini	Cancer	Leo	Virgo	Libra	Scorpio	Sagittarius	Capricorn	Aquarius	Pisces
Colour	Red	White	Green	Yellow	Red	Vegetable greenish	Black	Black – Red	Warm Grey (Dove-like)	Black	Earthly	Reddish White
Tempera-ment	Fiery	Earthly	Windy	Watery	Fiery	Earthly	Windy	Watery	Fiery	Earthly	Windy	Watery
Charac-teristics	Dry	Dry	Dry	Wet	Dry	Dry	Wet	Wet	Dry	Wet	Wet	Wet
Part of Body	Head	Neck	Arms	Chest	Stomach	Waist	Below Navel	Sex organs	Hips	Thighs	Feet	Lower position of foot
Height	Short Stature	Short Stature	Normal height	Normal height	Tall	Tall	Tall	Tall	Normal height	Normal height	Short Stature	Short Stature
Directions	East	South	West	North	East	South	West	North	East	South	West	North
Male or Female (Sex)	Male	Female	Male	Female	Male	Female	Male	Female	Male	Female	Male	Female
Nature	Bitter	Balanced	Bitter	Balanced	Bitter	Balanced	Bitter	Balanced	Bitter	Balanced	Bitter	Balanced
Mobile or Immobile	Mobile	Immobile	Partially mobile	Mobile	Immobile	Partially mobile	Mobile	Immobile	Partially mobile	Mobile	Immobile	Partially mobile

Contd...

[145]

Name of Sign	Aries	Taurus	Gemini	Cancer	Leo	Virgo	Libra	Scorpio	Sagittarius	Capricorn	Aquarius	Pisces
Lord Planet	Mars	Venus	Mercury	Moon	Sun	Mercury	Venus	Mars	Jupiter	Saturn	Saturn	Jupiter
Colour of Planet	Red	White	Green	Pearly White	Red	Green	White	Red (Blood)	Yellow	Black	Black	Yellow
Exalted Sign (Raashi) of Planet	Capricorn (10)	Pisces (12)	Virgo (6)	Taurus (2)	Aries (1)	Virgo (6)	Pisces (12)	Capricorn (10)	Cancer (4)	Libra (7)	Libra (7)	Cancer (4)
Debilitated Sign (Raashi) of Planet	Cancer (4)	Virgo (6)	Pisces (12)	Scorpio (8)	Libra (7)	Pisces (12)	Virgo (6)	Cancer (4)	Capricorn (10)	Aries (1)	Aries (1)	Capricorn (10)
Planet's stay in a Raashi	1½ Month	1 Month	1 Month	2¼ Month	1 Month	1 Month	1 Month	45 days	13 Months	30 Months	30 Months	13 Months

9. Chart showing Moon's effect in the Birth Chart:

After preparing the Birth chart, find out in which Sign (Raashi), Moon is situated and which planet fully aspects it (100% aspect). The effect of the planet which aspects it, is indicated in the chart below:

100% Aspects of Planets on Moon:

Name of Sign (Raashi)	Aries	Taurus	Gemini	Cancer	Leo	Virgo	Libra	Scorpio	Sagittarius	Capricorn	Aquarius	Pisces
Moon	Moon	Moon	Moon	Moon	Moon	Moon	Moon	Moon	Moon	Moon	Moon	Moon
Sun	Poor	Slave	Happy in poverty	Bad eye-sight	Brave	Short lived	Involved in troubles	Poor	Miserly slave	Hopeless	Peevish	Lustful
Mars	Exalted status	Poor	Fond of arms & ammunition	Brave	Exalted position	Marital discord	Fear of death	Exalted position	Back biter	Eminent status	Lustful, scoundrel	Lustful
Mercury	Scholar	Thief	Rich	Justice loving	Astrologer	Minister	Lustful	Two fathers	Clever & shrewd	Eminent status	Exalted status	Clown or jester
Jupiter	Exalted status	Name & Fame	Scholar	Scholar	Fortunate	Leader	Well dressed	Simple living	Fortunate	Eminent Status	Lucky	Exalted status
Venus	Skillful	Exalted status	Clever & cunning	Land Lord	Officer	Actor	Rich	Engraver architect	Famous	Wise	Luxurious life	Learned person
Saturn	Thief	Rich	Thief	Iron merchant	Mean profession	Marital discord	Full of troubles	Ugly	Bad at heart, minded evil	Rich	Lustful	Lustful, bad character

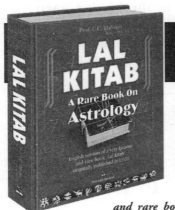

LAL KITAB
A Rare Book On Astrology

*English version of a very famous
and rare book 'Lal Kitab', originally published in Urdu*

A book on Astrology – Horoscope Reading Made Easy – was published in 2000 by Pustak Mahal, authored by Prof. U.C. Mahajan. The English version of Lal Kitab is an extension of the earlier book and both complement each other. Renowned astrologer, Roop Lal wrote Lal Kitab in Urdu, during the 19th century, based on an ancient text.

The salient points of this book are:

1. Every planet has a benefic or malefic effect according to its raashi and placement in a particular house. For example, Jupiter in house no.1 can exercise good or bad effects according to its nature, whether excellent or debilitating. Consequently, the author has classified the effect of every planet – good or bad – separately. The earlier book carried a generalised interpretation. Now, readers will find it easy to comprehend every planet's effect.

2. More case studies have been added to make it broad-based.

3. New chapters on a house, the effect of auspicious and inauspicious planets, precious stones and their significance, characteristics of all planets, nakshatras and their importance, Natal Moon chart and Saturn's transit (*Saade-Saati*) i.e., 7½ years of Saturn's malefic transit through the Moon, have been added.

4. Preparation of birth chart according to south Indian traditions has also been included.

*Size: 7.25"x9.5" • Pages: 336 (Hardbound)
Price: Rs. 295/- • Postage: Rs. 25/-*